Old-Fashioned Christmas Favorites

A heart-warming collection of treasured recipes, memories, handmade gifts, cozy decorating tips & easy how-to's for the joyous days of Christmas.

THE BEST OF
Gooseberry
Patch co.

Old-Fashioned Christmas Favorites

A heart-warming collection of treasured recipes, memories, handmade gifts, cozy decorating tips & easy how-to's for the joyous days of Christmas.

FRIEDMAN/FAIRFAX
PUBLISHERS

A FRIEDMAN/FAIRFAX BOOK

Text and Illustrations © 1997 by Gooseberry Patch

Library of Congress Cataloging-in-Publication Data

Martin, Jo Ann.
    The best of Gooseberry Patch : old-fashioned Christmas favorites :
    a heart-warming collection of treasured recipes, memories, handmade
    gifts, cozy decorating tips & easy how-to's for the joyous days of
    Christmas. / Jo Ann Martin, Vickie Hutchins.
        p. cm.
    ISBN 1-56799-537-3
    1. Christmas decorations. 2. Christmas cookery.   I. Hutchins, Vickie.
    II. Gooseberry Patch (Firm)   III. Title.
TT900.C4M293 1997
745.594'12—dc21   97-10733

Project Editor: Sharyn Rosart
Editor: Francine Hornberger
Art Director: Jeff Batzli
Design: Elan Studio
Production Director: Karen Matsu Greenberg

Color separations by Bright Arts Graphics (S) Pte Ltd.
Printed in England by Butler & Tanner Limited

1 3 5 7 9 10 8 6 4 2

For bulk purchases and special sales, please contact:
Friedman/Fairfax Publishers
Attention: Sales Department
15 West 26th Street
New York, New York 10010
212/685-6610   FAX 212/685-1307

Visit our website:
http://www.metrobooks.com

Contents

Acknowledgments ★ 6

Introduction ★ 8

Chapter One: Deck the Halls ★ 12

Chapter Two: Handmade with Love ★ 22

Chapter Three: Heartwarming Memories
and Traditions from Our Readers ★ 44

Chapter Four: Festive Foods for Holiday Feasts ★ 68

Chapter Five: Holiday Menus ★ 110

Index ★ 142

Acknowledgments

Our thanks to each one of you who shared your family traditions, recipes, and favorite holiday tips and ideas…you made this book possible. We continue to be overwhelmed by your response and generosity in welcoming us into your lives and sharing with us your warmest and most treasured Christmas memories. To all of you who have shared your thoughts and suggestions with us at **Gooseberry Patch** over the years, and whose names do not appear here, our heartfelt thanks for your contributions.

Peg Ackerman
Shirley Ainsworth
Pat Akers
Kristin Ammermann
Karen Antonides
Linda Arndt
Lorraine Athanosios
Rose Ayraud
Jackie Bankovic
Karyl Bannister

Barbara Bargdill
Carrol Begley
Yvonne Bendler
Sheri Berger
Cheryl Berry
Jennifer Bolton
Kathy Bolyea
Judy Borecky
Juliene Bramer
Theresa Brazil
Teresa Breitenstein
Sally Burke
Betty Byrd
Judy Carter
Suzanne Charland
Kathy Christianson
Margaret Clark
Debbie Clement
Patty Sue Cooper
Donna Crawford
Charlotte Crockett
Alfreda Crosley

Deb Damari-Tull
Joy Daniel
Ann Davis
Linda Day
Leslie Deatrich
Terrolee DeMenge
Diane Dollak
Deborah Donovan
Patricia Donza
Jo Carol Driver
Lisa Embree
Jeanine English
Janice Ertola

Kim Estes
Cheryl Ewer
Anne Farnese
Candace Faw
Ann Fehr
Elenna Firme
Marjorie Foland
Cindy Footit
Diann Fox
Elizabeth Fox
Mary Garramone
Paul Gaulke

Arlynn Geers
Nancie Gensler
Lisa Glenn
Myra Golubski
Netta Groat
Tamara Gruber
Pat Habiger
Charmaine Hahl
Doris Hammer
Judy Hand
Merideth Haus
Heather Hazen
Glenda Hill
Kathy Hill
Elizabeth Heyman
Peg Huffman
Patricia Husek
Joanne A. Jacobellis
Mickey Johnson
Charlene Julian
Judy Kelly
Mary Kelly

Debbie Kephart
Mary-Gail King
Patricia Kinghorn
Debbi Kinsey
Susan Kirschenheiter
Georgene Kornreich
Jan Kouzes
Teresa Labat
Pat LaFlame
Kathy Lafleur
Jacqueline Lash-Idler
Cindy Layton
Carolyn Ritz Lemon
Patricia Loughren
Janie Lusk
Joleen Lutz
Tina Main
Cathy Marcquenski
Sally McArthur
Barbara McCaffrey
Corinne McClellan
Barb McFadden

Debbie Meyer
Chris Montgomery
Mary Murray
Cheryl Neff
Joyce Newburn
ReDonna Newman
Sherry Obenauf
Cathrin Owens
Wendy Lee Paffenroth
Deborah Peters
Marion Pfeifer
Kathleen Popp
Brenda Radzinski
Terrie Rasmussen
Cynthia Reda
Andrea Redeker
Betty Richmond
Margaret Riley
Karen Roberts
Rosina Robinson

Michele Roudebush
Trudy Jo Snader
Jan Sofranko
Doris Stegner
Martha Terrell
Linda Tittle
Brenda Umphress
Michele Urdahl
Sheryl Valentine
Yvonne Van Brimmer
Charla Viehe
DiAnn Voegele
Beverlee Wallace
Cindy Wattenschaidt
Juanita Williams
Pauline Williams
Mel Wolk
Doodles Young
Aundra Zack
Lynda Zimmer

Introduction

Dear Friends,

A cherished gift to yourself or a dear friend, **Old-Fashioned Christmas Favorites** creates a delectable and delightful feast for the holidays! Come on in and share holiday recipes, decorating ideas, easy how-to's, loving memories, and family traditions. Whether the centerpiece of your holiday feast is **Grandma Essie Hill's Blackberry Cobbler** or **The Best Apple Walnut Raisin Pie**, let us share our bounty of time-treasured holiday recipes to ensure the happiest, most festive Yuletide season ever.

Enjoy the mouth-watering aroma of **Banny's Southern Cream Cookies** or relax with a quick-to-fix delicious dinner after a full day of

shopping. Create your own gift tags, ornaments, wrapping paper, holiday candles,
and scented bath salts. Decorating can
be as simple as preserving precious little
mittens now outgrown or collecting old
chandelier prisms to personalize your
holiday tree and make it sparkle. Fabric
gift bags or baskets filled with cookie cutters and homemade jellies create the best kind
of gift…homemade and from the heart.

Old-Fashioned Christmas Favorites

captures the whimsy and magic of all of the
books we've published, with the help of our
many friends from around the country.
Curl up with your favorite quilt by the
fire, relax, and join us as the celebra-
tion that is Christmas is about to
unfold…once more. Sharing…it's
what Christmas is all about!

With Christmas cheer,

Vickie & JoAnn

chapter one **Deck the Halls**

Trimming the Tree

Little mittens that have been outgrown look precious hanging on the Christmas tree.

Let your kids help you decorate your tree with memories of childhood...a dolly chain! Take a piece of sturdy paper, about 16 inches long and 5 inches high. Pleat the paper strip into fanfolds about 2 inches wide. Fasten pleats together with paper clips at the top and bottom. Draw one-half of a doll silhouette onto your paper. Using sharp scissors, cut out the shape. Make as many chains as desired and tape together. Spray with gold paint, or let the kids color the dolls for you.

String popcorn and cranberries on dental floss to decorate the Christmas tree. Thread a large sewing needle with waxed floss; it's very strong and the wax helps the popcorn and berries slide on easily. After the holidays, put the berry/popcorn garland on small trees or bushes as a special treat for the birds.

Make snowballs for your tree or mantel. Coat clear glass ball ornaments with white glue, or spray with adhesive. Then roll them in glitter until completely covered and hang the balls to dry. This is a great kids' project!

Be on the lookout for chandelier prisms at antique shops and flea markets. They make beautiful icicle ornaments for your tree or windows, or hanging from a mantelpiece garland.

For everyone in your family, make personalized ornaments with colored glass balls and glitter fabric paints in tubes. Use the paint to write names and messages on the balls, then finish decorating with paint, cording, jewels, sequins, and beads. Add a big bow to the top of the ball. At your family Christmas gathering, each person can take a turn hanging his or her ornament. Be sure to make new ornaments for new family members. It's a great way to welcome a new son- or daughter-in-law…or baby!… to the family.

Put the Christmas tree lights on a timer switch. That way you're not crawling over gifts Christmas Eve or morning to get the lights plugged in.

Tiny willow baskets, available at most craft and import shops, are just right for painting. A light coat of gold spray paint gives them a sheen, yet allows the woven texture to show through. After they've dried, fill them with foil-wrapped kisses or coins for good luck. Finish with a gold fabric bow, a tiny pinecone, and a sprig of greenery. Hang one for each member of your family on the tree.

During the year, purchase holiday cookie cutters (especially when on sale). Using red, green, or plaid ribbon as a "hanger," display them on your tree. As holiday guests leave, give each a cookie cutter along with a copy of your favorite cookie recipe as a little token of a special time spent together.

Hang holiday cookie cutters with ribbon at your windows for a special touch. Tuck in a scoop of holiday potpourri tied in a piece of netting or lace to enjoy the "smells of the season."

For a very special effect, throw popcorn on your Christmas tree. This gives the look of freshly fallen snow!

A Christmas tree without popcorn and cranberry strings just isn't a Christmas tree.

String dried apple and orange slices for your country Christmas tree. Simply loop a piece of twine through the slice, hang, and enjoy. It is also fun to dust the dried apples with cinnamon. They make the tree look and smell wonderful.

★ ★ ★ ★ ★ ★ ★ ★ ★ ★ ★ ★ ★ ★ ★ ★ ★ ★

Make your own potpourri using dried apple slices, bay leaves, cinnamon sticks, and nutmegs, and display in the glass globe of an old lantern. Finish off with a bow and greenery around the bottom for a great centerpiece. You can also make garlands for use all year long with the same materials. When decorating your kitchen for the holidays, hang the garlands in your kitchen windowsill or across the outside back of ladderback chairs.

Don't forget to take photographs of the everyday joys of the holidays. Take pictures of family members occupied with the tasks they enjoy…Dad stringing the outside lights, the kids rolling out cookie dough, Mom wrapping presents, cozy pictures of the family just curling up by the fire. Pictures bring back the fondest memories.

At Christmastime I put together gingerbread families for all my grandchildren. I have a Mama, Papa, sister, and brothers, along with pet bears or dogs, and each one has a tiny red satin ribbon tied around its neck. I pack these "families" in Christmas tins or colorful small paper bags. Who says children shouldn't play with their food?

Does your tree look "lonely" before and after the presents? Arrange your children's stuffed animals or dolls to sit beneath it until the packages arrive or you take down the tree.

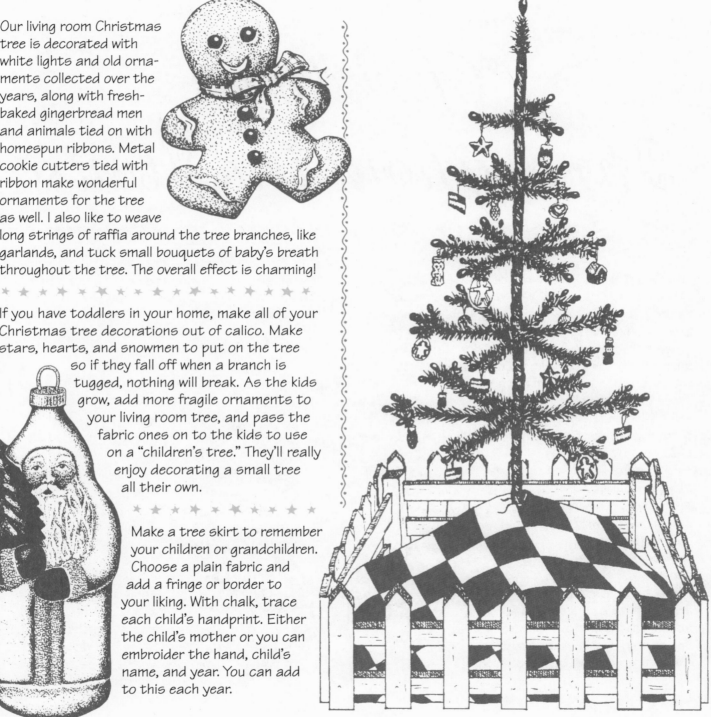

Our living room Christmas tree is decorated with white lights and old ornaments collected over the years, along with fresh-baked gingerbread men and animals tied on with homespun ribbons. Metal cookie cutters tied with ribbon make wonderful ornaments for the tree as well. I also like to weave long strings of raffia around the tree branches, like garlands, and tuck small bouquets of baby's breath throughout the tree. The overall effect is charming!

* *

If you have toddlers in your home, make all of your Christmas tree decorations out of calico. Make stars, hearts, and snowmen to put on the tree so if they fall off when a branch is tugged, nothing will break. As the kids grow, add more fragile ornaments to your living room tree, and pass the fabric ones on to the kids to use on a "children's tree." They'll really enjoy decorating a small tree all their own.

* * * * * * * * * * * * * *

Make a tree skirt to remember your children or grandchildren. Choose a plain fabric and add a fringe or border to your liking. With chalk, trace each child's handprint. Either the child's mother or you can embroider the hand, child's name, and year. You can add to this each year.

Christmas Throughout the House

The natural beauty of colorful citrus will enhance your holiday home! Dry your citrus slices several weeks before you make your garland. Slice lemons, oranges, and limes crosswise into ¼-inch slices. Spread the slices on racks or paper towels to dry, turning frequently. (We don't recommend newspaper, as the ink sometimes transfers to the slices.) When the slices are dry but still pliable and "leathery," string them onto dental floss alternately with whole cinnamon sticks and red wooden beads. Make the garland as long as you need for hanging across a window. For a different effect, begin with a red wooden bead and string short, uneven lengths of slices, cinnamon, and beads, ending with a loop. Hook the loop directly over a curtain rod, or use ornament hangers to hang it over the rod. String an evergreen garland along the top of the rod to cover the ends of your garland.

If you have never made greenery wreaths before, it's something you should try. My husband and I have been making them since our first Christmas. We go into the woods one week before Thanksgiving and fill two large burlap bags full of greens. (Leave them outside in the cold to keep them fresh and green.) After Thanksgiving, the fun of making the wreaths begins! To make your wreath, tie bunches of greens onto a wire wreath, which can be purchased at a craft store. Follow the outside circle, then do the inside circle. Place a hook on the back and a big red bow on the front. I have fun decorating the outside of my house with the wreaths. It gives the house a real old-fashioned country Christmas look.

It's fun and easy to make pretty paper snow-flakes for hanging in your windows all through the winter. Just take a piece of heavy white paper and cut it into a square. Then fold several times. Use scissors to cut the folded paper into various shapes such as triangles, squares, and diamonds. When you unfold the paper, you'll have a beautiful design. Carefully press with a warm iron to remove the creases. Then have fun decorating your snowflakes! Use gold or silver metallic spray paint, or cover with glitter or sequins. Your kids will love coloring them with markers, then adding sparkly glitter with glue. Just punch a hole in the top of each snowflake and they're ready for hanging…in windows, on your mantel, in mirrors, on a large plant, on your Christmas tree, above a doorway…anywhere at all.

* * * * * * * * * * * * * * * *

Cut out of green felt or a green tablecloth the outline of a Christmas tree (make it large enough to fit on a door or a wall). Take Christmas cookie cutters and trace outlines on poster board or other heavy paper. Cut out the shapes. Place the shapes in a basket with crayons and a roll of tape. When little visitors come to your home, or on days when nothing will entertain your children, let them color the shapes and affix them to the tree.

Frame an indoor doorway with evergreen garlands decorated with gingerbread figures, dried apples, cinnamon sticks, and homespun ribbons. Include Christmas tree lights with the garlands.

* * * * * * * * * * * * * * * *

Use Christmas dishes instead of everyday dishes throughout the year to keep the magic of the holidays alive year-round.

* * * * * * * * * * * * * * * *

Play Christmas tapes and records collected over the years constantly throughout December, especially the instrumentals that might have been heard during the eighteenth and nineteenth centuries. These give a wonderful "old-time" atmosphere to the holidays.

Over the river and through the wood,
To grandmother's house we go;
The horse knows the way
To carry the sleigh,
Through the white and drifted snow
Over the river and through the wood,
Oh how the wind does blow;
It stings the toes
And bites the nose,
As over the ground we go.
—Lydia Maria Child

Decorate your mailbox for Christmas with a fresh wreath or a spray of Christmas greenery and a big red bow you can reuse each year.

＊ ＊ ＊ ＊ ＊ ＊ ＊ ＊ ＊ ＊ ＊ ＊ ＊ ＊ ＊ ＊

Choose a special decorating theme each Christmas that you can coordinate throughout the house. For a natural theme, string a greenery garland on your front porch and along the railing of your back porch.

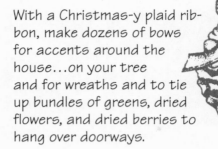

With a Christmas-y plaid ribbon, make dozens of bows for accents around the house…on your tree and for wreaths and to tie up bundles of greens, dried flowers, and dried berries to hang over doorways.

＊ ＊ ＊ ＊ ＊ ＊ ＊ ＊ ＊ ＊ ＊ ＊ ＊ ＊ ＊

For my holiday decorations, I like to use some of my favorite antiques and lots of greenery tied with bright ribbons. I place garlands on the stairway, and fill a large copper bowl on my dining room table with pinecones and greens. By my front door, I place an old sled with a pair of old ice skates and a tiny pair of old mittens hanging on it. I think the natural things that we live with make the most beautiful decorations if you have a bit of imagination.

＊ ＊ ＊ ＊ ＊ ＊ ＊ ＊ ＊ ＊ ＊ ＊ ＊ ＊

Take the branch trimmings from the tree and put into vases, pitchers, mugs, and other containers. Add artificial red berries, then hang small colored glass balls. This really brings the Christmas spirit to every room in the house. It's like having a mini Christmas tree for every room. The "bouquet" in the kitchen can have small cookie cutters tied on with red ribbon, too!

＊ ＊ ＊ ＊ ＊ ＊ ＊ ＊ ＊ ＊ ＊ ＊ ＊ ＊

Place lots of pure white votive candles in glass holders on the mantel and all over the house to add an overall twinkly light.

At Christmastime, add a festive ribbon to jars of potpourri and line them up on the mantel, or on a shelf on the bookcase, where the glass sparkles and catches the light.

Special touches for guest rooms include fresh flowers, electric tea kettle, china cups, a basket of special teas and instant coffees, fresh fruit, magazines, and extra quilts and cozy blankets.

Line the front and back stairs with poinsettias and alternate with Teddy bears. You could also cover the poinsettia pots with bags and tie with raffia and cinnamon hearts.

For a festive entrance, pot small live trees, such as Norfolk pines, in straw baskets. Wrap the baskets in big red ribbons and place them by your front door.

Tuck silverware into clean, brightly colored mittens at each place setting. Use a scarf as a table runner for a warm wintertime gathering.

To make a whimsical festive centerpiece, use apples and taper candles. Select apples that stand on end well. Core them three-quarters of the way through and place a taper candle in the center of each apple. Place three or four apples down the center of the table and fill in with holly and greenery.

Mark guests' places with personalized ornaments tied with a bow and placed in wine glasses. Write their names on the ornaments with acrylic paints or a gold or silver pen.

When you visit a china store that has inexpensive plates or platters, purchase several to use for special homemade gifts of food. Large platters with an array of cookies or bread slices, decorated with fresh greens and berries, are a beautiful and most thoughtful gift of friendship. Wrap them in pretty cellophane, tie with fabric ribbon and bows, and give to friends and neighbors during the holidays.

Fill your kitchen with Christmas… decorate a kitchen tree! Use your smallest kitchen utensils, gingham bows, and tiny cookie cutters as decorations. Or, try gingerbread cookies and cinnamon sticks tied with red bows. Yet another variation could be fragrant herb bundles, dried flowers, and baby's breath with silk ribbons. Beautiful kitchen tree toppers could be a gingerbread angel or star, a small tin cookie cutter, a chef's hat trimmed with holly and berries, a country crow wearing a Christmas bow, a little wooden spoon angel, or a handmade rag angel made from a new dishcloth. If there isn't room for a kitchen tree, or if very young children abound, consider using a smaller, tabletop version…or hang a kitchen wreath using these decorating ideas. It's a fun way to fill your kitchen with the sights and scents of Christmas.

Ice ornaments make interesting outdoor tree decorations as they twist and sparkle in the wind. Line the inside edge of an aluminum pie pan with yarn, leaving enough yarn loose at the top to tie around a tree branch. Fill the tin with water and add berries, flowers, and greenery to the water. Place the pans on a level surface in the freezer or outside if the temperature is below freezing. Freeze the pan until everything inside is frozen solid. Remove the ice from the pan (you may have to dip briefly in warm water) and hang outside to enjoy.

If the headboard on your bed is a tall one, why not decorate it with a garland?

Pick one room in which to do all your Christmas wrapping and crafting. Don't worry about keeping it tidy. Wrap the door to look like a package with a sign that reads "Do not open until Christmas," or "Santa's Workshop," or "Do Not Enter... Authorized Elves Only!"

* * * * * * * * * * * * * * * * * * *

Don't forget your pets at Christmas. Hang a wreath on the doghouse. How about lights? Put a little jingle bell on Queenie's collar, or a Christmas bandanna around Sammy's neck.

* * * * * * * * * * * * * * * * * * *

When everything is cold and snowy, it's so wonderful and festive to have potted flowers growing inside. Narcissus and amaryllis bulbs are plentiful this time of year, and it's amazing to watch their incredible growth...a bit of springtime almost right before your eyes! For a bit of color and good cheer, pick up a Christmas cactus, cyclamen, violet, or gloxinia.

* * * * * * * * * * * * * * * * * * *

Send a Christmas "care" package to a child who's away at college. Include a small Christmas tree, ornaments, a tape of holiday music, a batch of their favorite holiday cookies... whatever would make their holiday more merry. This is sure to be a big hit!

This might be the first year the reindeer leave carrot "crumbs" on the front lawn. Surprise your kids by putting shredded carrots all over the lawn.

String tiny colored lights on an outside tree, bringing the Christmas spirit out to the backyard as well as inside. Turn the lights on in the afternoon and have fun watching the birds sit in the tree among the twinkling lights.

* * * * * * * * * * * * * * * * * * *

Candy canes and silverware tied with a Christmas bow are a delightful surprise greeting at a holiday table.

Country Crafts

Mini-Cookbook Greeting Cards

I've always included a recipe with my Christmas cards. A few years ago I decided to do a mini-cookbook Christmas card. Here's how you can make your own:

- Take a sheet of typing paper and fold it into quarters. When cut, this will make an 8-page cookbook. If a 16-page cookbook is desired, use two sheets of paper.
- Type your recipes and have your local copy shop reduce them to fit the size of the pages. (If you've used an 8½" × 11" sheet of paper, your cookbook pages will be 4¼" × 5½" after folding.)
- Next, cut out the printed recipes and glue them onto the pages with a glue stick. So that your recipes are placed correctly, make up a dummy copy of your book before you start. Get as creative as you like by decorating borders around your recipes, if you choose. Another fun idea is to use rubber stamps to add lots of country charm after your book is assembled. Decorate the front panel as the greeting page.
- Now it's time to photocopy your pages. Make as many copies as you will need, and remember to copy on both sides of each sheet so that your recipes will be back to back and going in the right direction.
- Cut your pages in half and carefully machine sew up the center of the card to hold your pages in place. You can then flip through the pages to see all your wonderful recipes!

This is a fun and really inexpensive way to share some favorite recipes with loved ones. The only problem is that once you start sending recipe greeting cards, your family and friends won't let you stop. Mine tell me they look forward to my "Christmas Calories" every year and it's a card that is never thrown away.

Yuletide Potpourri

2 c. pine needles
3 T. rosemary
dried orange peel
tiny pinecones
1 c. bay leaves
1 T. whole cloves
cinnamon sticks
berries
2 T. ground
    orris root
14 drops
    cinnamon oil

Mix the first eight ingredients in a ceramic or glass bowl. In a separate container, stir together the ground orris root and cinnamon oil. Add this to the dried mixture. Toss gently. Allow to cure for two weeks in a tightly closed container in a cool, dark place. Shake occasionally.

Soap Stars

You will need a fresh bar of snowy-white soap and a standard cheese slicer. Wet the slicer and slice the soap lengthwise, making the pieces about ¼-inch thick. Lay the slice of soap on a flat work surface. Wet a star cookie cutter and press into the soap. Lift and gently remove the star from the cookie cutter. Return star to the flat work surface. With an awl or ice pick, punch a hole for string or ribbon to pass through. Red gingham is also festive. These stars are great for the tree, wreaths, or even as guest soaps.

Bundle branches of white pine, cedar, and winterberry, and tie them together with raffia for a country touch.

Tweet Hearts

You can give your feathered friends a treat this holiday season by following this simple recipe.

1¼ lbs. suet
½ c. crushed peanuts
½ c. sunflower seeds
½ c. cracked corn kernels

Melt suet in oven or saucepan (yields about 2 cups liquid fat). Stir in peanuts, sunflower seeds, and corn. Spoon mixture into four one-cup heart molds; insert a drinking straw at top (for hole). Cool in the refrigerator until solid. Unmold, remove straw, thread with string, and tie to a shaded tree branch.

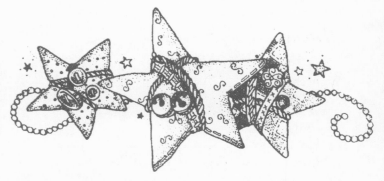

Be prepared ahead of time with gifts
for friends who drop by during the holidays.
Wonderful gifts straight from the heart might
include: holiday cups and gourmet coffee, teas,
cocoas, and gingerbread men; cookie cutters
with your favorite Christmas cookie recipe
attached; or handmade ornaments.

Light fades
Stars appear
Evening angels
gather here

Family Treasures

Each year, give your children a special gift in a
frame. It might be an enlarged family photograph,
a special piece of artwork from school, or a
favorite poster. Write a message on the back of
the framed piece before you wrap it. This way, when
your children grow up and leave home, they will
have special family treasures to take with them.

Dried Cranberry Heart

To make a dried cranberry heart, use a fine-gauge
wire and a strong craft needle to string the cranberries. Then shape the wire into a heart. To make
a more substantial heart-shaped decoration,
make several strings of cranberries, place them
together, and tie with twisted pieces of wire. Top
with a piece of homespun fabric tied with some
sprigs of pine. Hang on the kitchen wall or along
your mantel.

Take a walk in the woods and collect
pinecones, moss, pine, evergreen, nuts, and
pods, and fill a big basket or bowl!

Framed Picture Ornaments

Here's a great project for the kids. Save the shiny metal lids from frozen juice cans. During the year, set aside their best little photos, such as those taken at school or on their birthdays. (Double prints are great!) Take out the photos and cut the images to fit inside the lids. Help them glue some rickrack, ribbon, or lace around the edge, and glue a loop of pretty fabric ribbon to the back...you'll have a Christmas ornament for Grandma and Grandpa. Or, if you'd rather, buy some disk magnets in the craft section and glue them onto the backs of the lids. Then the relatives can look at their little angels all year 'round, every time they go to the fridge!

Fabric Gift Bags

Take a piece of burlap, fold it to the size you need, then trim and sew up the sides to resemble a sack. Sew a drawstring hem into the top and thread it with bright red yarn. On the side of the bag, stencil a Christmas design such as holly and a Santa with acrylic paint. Tuck any gift you please inside the bag, and stuff it with mounds of bright tissue or paper shreddings. They'll be able to use the bag over and over again.

Take leftover Christmas fabric and make it into a small bag. Don't worry about the top; you don't have to finish it...just gather it together and tie it with ribbon. Inside the bag, fit a very tiny box of earrings or a pin. Your friends will want to save the "Christmas Bag" and use it next year for a gift they give to someone else.

Family Fun Surprise Jar

Cut Christmas wrapping paper into 3-inch squares. On the blank side of each square, have family members write ideas for fun things the family can do together during the holidays. Examples might be watching last year's video, sledding, making hot chocolate and popcorn, or driving around looking at Christmas lights. Then fold the papers with the wrapping-paper side showing and place them all in a large jar. Each day agree to draw one idea, then do the activity together. This gives your family some quality sharing time together each day throughout the holiday season. Enjoy, and Merry Christmas!

Grandparents' Gifts

Have your children make and decorate their own Christmas cards shaped as Santa, a Christmas tree, gingerbread house, or such. Inside, paste a picture of the child or the child with grandparent. Then have the child write a sentence and sign. It will become a treasured gift and could even be framed.

Teens can be particularly hard to buy for. Here are some great ideas: CDs, cassettes, sporting goods, magazine subscriptions, movie passes, blank cassettes, concert tickets, batteries, art supplies, and gift certificates for videos, video game rentals, arcades, or bookstores.

Gift Tags

You may find that many commercial gift tags are too small for your use. If so, you can make your own using blank 3" × 5" cards. Just fold them in half and decorate with some Christmas fabric, wrapping paper, or cut-up Christmas cards. With a little white glue, stick the picture or decoration on the front. Use a hole punch and put a hole in the corner and tie on some ribbon. The ideas are endless. Let the kids do this over the Thanksgiving holidays or on a snowy day.

These also make great ornaments tied onto your tree.

Scented Bath Salts

Make your own bath salts in your favorite scents. Use plain rock salt and add a few drops of essential oil. Lavender and rose work really well. Bottle the salts up in pretty jars or other containers for unique and inexpensive gifts. Be sure to make your bath salts a few weeks ahead of time to allow the oil to thoroughly scent the salts. Write a little homemade tag with the simple instructions: Place a few tablespoons of bath salts under the faucet as you draw your bath.

One of our friends from Maine taught us something new this year. She packs her gift shipments with pinecones. They're much better than Styrofoam or wadded-up plastic shopping bags. Not only do they protect your gifts, but they look Christmas-y, can be reused as decorations, and they're better for the environment. Make sure the pinecones are dry and opened, so no sap is running.

Scented Pinecone Baskets

Take the kids pinecone hunting…gather as many pinecones as you can find to fill baskets, then sprinkle with potpourri scents. Tie on ribbons and share them with friends and neighbors.

Holiday Candles

Make your own herbal candles for a fraction of what they cost in specialty shops. Purchase pillar candles. Sage green and ecru colors work best. Prepare a mixture of spices such as rosemary, sage, and thyme or cinnamon, nutmeg, and ground cloves. Melt inexpensive paraffin and dip your candles into the melted wax. Immediately roll them in the desired spice mixture. Using your hands, press the spices into the warm wax. Repeat the process several times to create a nubby-textured candle. A spice candle looks beautiful in a wooden, yellowware, or graniteware bowl with bay leaves and rose hips surrounding it.

Here's a loving gift for your child straight from the heart. Assemble a recipe box with all Grandma's and Mom's favorite family recipes. Add new recipes each year along with funny little notes and sayings. A warm, wonderful gift to grow right along with your child…truly a box full of memories!

Twinkling Grapevine Spheres

Use up any spare grapevine you may have around. Soak the grapevine in warm water until pliable. Using a large round balloon that is inflated, gently wrap the grapevine around the balloon to form a sphere. Make it as dense or as sparse as you choose. Once the grapevine has dried, pop the balloon. These spheres look really magical wired with tiny twinkling white lights suspended from bare tree branches.

Candy Cane Door Prizes

Purchase mini candy canes in the long, clear cellophane wrappers (the kind that are usually hanging on display racks). Tie on red and green bows between the candy canes. Hang them on the wall by your front door, along with a small pair of scissors. As guests leave, cut off a candy cane for them to take with them. You can also do this with small homemade gingerbread men. Simply wrap them in a long strip of plastic.

Photo-Wrap

Make gift wrap out of your family photos. Take your pictures to your local printer and have them copied onto large sheets of paper. Use red raffia as your "ribbon." It's great for small packages! Copy the kids' pictures for Grandma. She'll love it. Print shops can now make full-color copies of photos. It's an easy way to add a family photo to your Christmas cards and letters.

Gift Box Advent Calendar

Here's how to make an Advent calendar for a friend to enjoy! Purchase 24 small, square white gift boxes at a box-and-mail specialty store. With a big marker, number each box on one side, numbers 1 through 24 (for the days in December that lead up to Christmas). Just for fun, vary the way you number them, using numeric symbols, Roman numerals, writing out the words, using foreign languages, and so on. Purchase small gifts to fit inside each box, such as a fast-food gift certificate, socks, small wind-up toys, movie money, special candy…whatever your friend would appreciate. Wrap each item in colorful tissue and slip each into its own box. Seal each box with a holiday sticker. Stack the boxes in order on their sides, with the numbers all facing forward. With a hot glue gun, glue the boxes together, and wrap wide red ribbon around the outside perimeter with a big bow on top. Give the calendar to your friend before December 1 so he or she can enjoy the anticipation. Each morning from December 1 to December 24, your friend will have the thrill of opening another box.

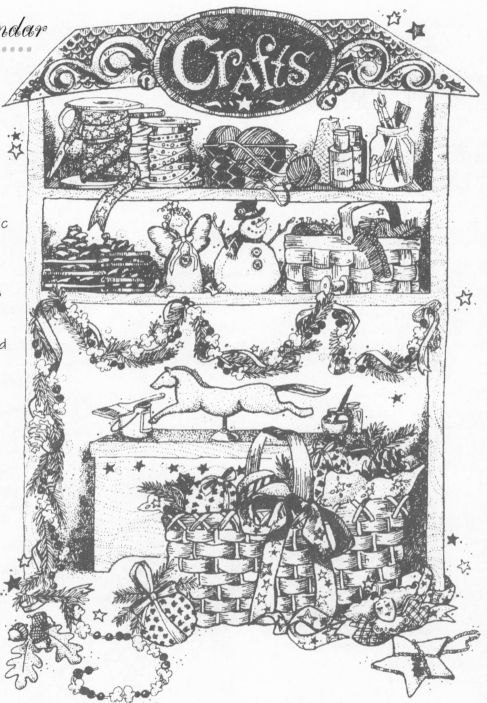

Have a Green Christmas

We should all be concerned about the earth and the environment and be thinking "green." To have an environmental Christmas, buy a good artificial tree that lasts for years. If you want to use a real tree, after Christmas, remove the tinsel and put the tree by your bird feeder as a shelter for the birds. You can also collect the pine needles for potpourri and mulch the tree when you're through with it.

How about some do-it-yourself Christmas wrap? Cut simple designs (hearts, trees, stars) out of sponges. Dip designs into acrylic paint, blot once on newspaper, and stamp out great designs on kraft or white shelf paper.

Themed Gift Baskets

I like to give homemade gifts to friends and family. One of my favorite things to do is buy an inexpensive basket and fill it with little things. I like to create a theme for each basket. If someone likes to write, I'll use stationery, note cards, pencils, and a book of stamps; another favorite is a bath basket with sponges, decorative soaps, pretty washcloths, lotion, and bath beads. I like to give goodie baskets too. I'll make a couple of batches of cookies and, knowing that a lot of people are health conscious now, I'll bake banana bread or cake in mini loaf pans or muffin tins. I divide the cookies into batches of four or five and also divide one large cheese ball into four or five mini cheese balls. I'll place all these goodies in a basket and tie with a big bow or place them in a pretty gift bag (Christmas, of course). This gives a sample of everything, without a lot of waste. They make nice hostess gifts. I've also added a "homemade" potpourri, which I make by purchasing a large bag of holiday potpourri and dividing it into four small clear plastic bags, tying a pretty ribbon at the top. Though the items themselves are simple, the thought that goes into each basket makes it a special gift.

Casserole Cozies

Make a fabric casserole cozy out of a quilted fabric place mat or a heavy, finished piece of fabric. Cut out the fabric around the dish and allow approximately one inch above the sides for hemming. Fit the corners around the casserole dish by pinching them together and sewing two buttons opposite each other on each of the four corners.

Potpourri Sachets

To decorate your country Christmas tree, you can make these easy potpourri sachets. They're very attractive, and they smell great! Choose your favorite fabric according to your theme...country gingham, tiny floral patterns, plaids, or checks. Cut the size according to the proportion of your tree; a 4" × 6" square will give you about a 3" × 5" bag. Put the right sides of the fabric together and just hand or machine-stitch each side and along the bottom. Leave the top unfinished for a more country look. Turn the bag inside out and fill with potpourri. Tie the top with ribbon or raffia. Attach any type of string or ribbon as a loop for hanging. These simple sachets make thoughtful, unique gifts.

Advent Chain

Your child can make an Advent chain. Help him or her glue together a paper chain, alternating with red and green construction paper. Make 25 links, and each day, beginning December 1st, tear off one link. This will help your child know how many days are left before Christmas, so the anticipation can build! This little poem can be attached to the top of the chain:

December 1st to Christmas is the longest time of year
Seems as though old Santa never will appear.
How many days to Christmas? It's mighty hard to count
So this little chain will tell you just the right amount.

Easy Christmas Tree Lapel Pin

Here's a fun project for kids…an easy gift they can make! You will need:

- assorted fabrics or grosgrain ribbons in pretty holiday colors
- a cinnamon stick
- a pin back from the jewelry section of a craft store
- hot glue
- special button

Be sure to select fabrics that have some stiffness and aren't too "floppy." Tear the fabric into small strips approximately ¼-inch wide. Simply tie the fabric strips onto the cinnamon stick. Once all the fabrics are tied on to suit you, snip the ends so that they're narrow at the top and wide at the bottom, shaped like a Christmas tree. Glue the pin back in place. You can decorate the top of your tree with a pretty gold, silver, or star-shaped button.

For unusual gift ribbons, shop your fabric store for remnants. Cut scraps of fabric like gingham, dotted Swiss, flannel, or velvet into strips to make unique package ties.

Potpourri Ornaments

Here's an easy idea that your friends will enjoy! Pick up some baby-sized woolen mittens or socks from a craft bazaar or baby store. Fill each mitten about two-thirds full with spicy potpourri and tie closed with twine, ribbon or yarn. Give as tree ornaments or as drawer sachets.

Gifts from the Kitchen

Gingerbread Babies

Tuck them into a little basket and leave them on someone's doorstep…surely you know someone who will give them a good home at Christmas!

½ c. butter, softened
¾ c. brown sugar, firmly packed
1 large egg
¼ c. dark molasses
2⅔ c. all-purpose flour
2 t. ginger
½ t. nutmeg
½ t. cinnamon
½ t. allspice
¼ t. salt

Preheat oven to 350°. In mixing bowl, beat butter and brown sugar until fluffy. Add egg and molasses. In separate bowl, stir together the dry ingredients. Gradually stir dry ingredients into the butter mixture. Turn dough out onto well-floured board and roll out to ⅛-inch thickness. Cut out lots of gingerbread babies and bake on a well-greased cookie sheet for 9 to 10 minutes. Makes 18 large gingerbread men or 50 babies.

Apricot Nut Bread

Wrap it up for your favorite hostess.

2¼ c. biscuit mix
1 c. quick oats
¾ c. sugar
1 t. baking powder
¼ t. salt
½ c. dried apricots, chopped
1 c. walnuts, chopped
1¼ c. milk
1 large egg, lightly beaten

Preheat oven to 350°. Combine dry ingredients in a bowl. Add fruit and nuts and mix to coat. Add remaining milk and egg, and stir just to moisten. Pour into a 9" × 5" × 3" loaf pan sprayed with nonstick spray. Bake for one hour. Test with a toothpick for doneness.

Holiday Gift Cakes

Make them as big or little as you want, and decorate accordingly. Wrap in brown paper tied with homespun or paper twist and a sprig of pine or holly.

8-oz. pkg. cream cheese, softened
1 c. (2 sticks) margarine, softened
1½ c. sugar
1½ t. vanilla
4 large eggs
2¼ c. sifted cake flour, divided
1½ t. baking powder
¾ c. (8-oz. jar) maraschino cherries
drained, chopped
½ c. pecans, chopped

Glaze:
1½ c. powdered sugar, sifted
2 T. milk

red or green maraschino cherries and pecan halves for decoration

Preheat oven to 325°. Thoroughly blend softened cream cheese, margarine, sugar, and vanilla. Add eggs, one at a time, mixing well after each addition. Sift 2 cups flour with baking powder. Gradually add sifted flour mixture to batter. Dredge chopped cherries and ½ cup chopped pecans with remaining ¼ cup flour; fold into batter. Grease a 10-inch bundt or tube pan; sprinkle with ½ cup finely chopped pecans. Pour batter into pan. Bake for one hour and 20 minutes, or until done. Cool 5 minutes; remove from pan. While cake is baking, prepare glaze; combine powdered sugar and milk. Add more milk, if needed for drizzling consistency. Drizzle glaze over top and sides of cake. Decorate with cherries and pecan halves, as desired.

Variations

For Christmas gifts, bake the cakes in ovenproof cans or other containers and omit the ½ cup finely chopped nuts for lining pans.

* * * * * *

Pour 2 cups batter into each of three greased one-pound coffee cans. Bake in a 325° oven one hour.

* * * * * *

Pour ½ cup batter into each of eleven greased 8-oz. tomato sauce cans. Bake in a 325° oven 25 minutes.

* * * * * *

Pour one cup batter into each of five greased 6" × 3½" loaf pans. Bake in a 325° oven 45 to 50 minutes.

A house is not beautiful because of its walls, but because of its cakes.
—Old Russian Proverb

Holiday Chocolate Bars

Cut these bars small…they are very rich.

1¾ c. unsifted all-purpose flour
½ c. sugar
¼ c. cocoa
½ c. chilled margarine
    or butter
1 large egg, beaten
14-oz. can sweetened
    condensed milk
12-oz. pkg. semisweet
    chocolate chips
1 c. nuts, chopped

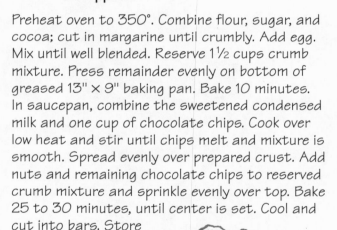

Preheat oven to 350°. Combine flour, sugar, and cocoa; cut in margarine until crumbly. Add egg. Mix until well blended. Reserve 1½ cups crumb mixture. Press remainder evenly on bottom of greased 13" × 9" baking pan. Bake 10 minutes. In saucepan, combine the sweetened condensed milk and one cup of chocolate chips. Cook over low heat and stir until chips melt and mixture is smooth. Spread evenly over prepared crust. Add nuts and remaining chocolate chips to reserved crumb mixture and sprinkle evenly over top. Bake 25 to 30 minutes, until center is set. Cool and cut into bars. Store covered at room temperature.

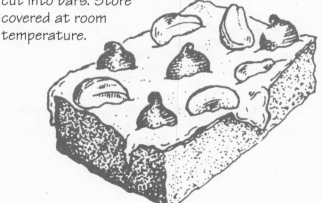

Peanut Brittle

I was church secretary for several years, and a batch of this peanut brittle was my first Christmas gift to the pastor. He always hinted for his peanut brittle when it got close to Christmas. When he was transferred to a church in another city, he told the new pastor to remember to hint for peanut brittle for Christmas…which he did!

2 c. sugar
1 c. dark corn syrup
1 c. water
1 lb. raw peanuts
2 T. butter or margarine
2 t. vanilla (premeasure so it's ready to add
    quickly)
2 t. baking soda (premeasure so it's ready
    to add quickly)

Mix sugar, corn syrup, and water in a large kettle. Cook covered until mixture boils, then remove cover. From now on stir to prevent burning, using a wooden spoon. When temperature reaches 236°, add peanuts. When temperature reaches 280°, add butter or margarine. When temperature reaches 300°, remove from heat and add vanilla and baking soda, stirring constantly. Pour immediately onto a large (no-sided) buttered cookie sheet. Do not try to spread too thin, peanut brittle is more crunchy if left a little thick. After peanut brittle hardens a few minutes, put a spatula under edges and loosen all around cookie sheet. Place in refrigerator for 30 minutes. When cool, remove and break into pieces and store in a covered container. This recipe may take a little longer to make than other peanut brittle recipes…about one hour from beginning to end… but it is well worth the extra time.

Homemade Caramels

Tuck these into a little wax paper–lined box and tie with a piece of homespun ribbon.

2 c. sugar
½ lb. butter
1½ c. dark sweet corn syrup
1 pt. cream, divided
nuts, optional
waxed paper

Place sugar, butter, corn syrup, and ½ pint cream in a large saucepan and bring to a boil. Add remaining ½ pint cream, bit by bit, never letting the syrup stop boiling until it reaches the hard ball stage at 245°. Add one teaspoon vanilla and nuts if desired. Pour into large shallow buttered pan. When cold, cut and wrap in wax paper.

Orange–Cranberry Marmalade

For a memorable gift, place this in a cute antique jar tied with a ribbon.

2 c. fresh cranberries
⅔ c. orange juice
2 t. grated orange peel
½ c. sugar

In a 2-quart saucepan, over high heat, combine all ingredients, bringing to a boil. Reduce heat to low, cover, and simmer until cranberries pop and mixture thickens slightly (about 20 minutes), stirring occasionally. Store in refrigerator in heat-proof jar. Makes 1½ cups.

Invite your friends to come over for a holiday dessert party. Serve several different desserts with coffee, brandy, and dessert wines. Fruit and cheese are nice accompaniments.

Hot Pepper Jelly

This looks "holiday special" and it tastes so good. Pack it with a wooden serving spoon. It's great with cream cheese and unsalted crackers.

1½ c. chopped green pepper, seeded
4-oz. can chili peppers, drained
6½ c. sugar
1½ c. cider vinegar
⅛ t. green food coloring
two 3-oz. pouches liquid fruit pectin

Put peppers and chilies in blender or food processor. Cover and process until puréed. In a stainless or enameled saucepan, heat sugar and vinegar until the sugar dissolves. Add pepper purée and bring to a boil over high heat. Reduce heat to moderately low and let simmer for 5 minutes. Stir in food coloring. Skim off and discard foam. Remove from heat and stir in pectin. Pour into eight ½-pint sterilized jars, filling each to within ⅛ inch of the top. Seal jars with lids and screw bands or rubber rings and clamp tops. Cool upright on wire racks. Makes about eight ½-pint jars.

Holiday Cocoa

A pair of mugs and a tin of holiday cookies would go nicely with this gift.

6 c. unsweetened cocoa
2 c. malted milk powder
7 c. sugar
2 T. cinnamon
1 vanilla bean, split in half

Blend all ingredients and let sit for three days. Spoon 3 cups into five gift jars. Include these instructions with your gift: Mix ¼ cup of mix into an 8- or 10-ounce mug of hot milk.

Date & Pumpkin Loaves

Mini loaves, fragrant with spices, make great hostess gifts.

3½ c. all-purpose flour
2 t. baking soda
1½ t. salt
1 t. cinnamon
1 t. nutmeg
1 t. allspice
3 c. sugar
1 c. oil
4 large eggs, beaten
⅔ c. water
2 c. (1 ½-lb. can) pumpkin
1¼ c. pecans, chopped
1 c. dates, chopped

Preheat oven to 350°. Combine dry ingredients and mix well. Combine wet ingredients and mix with dry ingredients. Add pecans and dates. Pour into three small greased loaf pans. Bake for one hour. Allow to sit several hours before slicing.

Gilded fruit and vegetables add sparkle and elegance to your holiday centerpieces. With gold spray paint, give a festive touch to artichokes, mini pumpkins, gourds, and pomegranates. Make sure you spray paint in a well-ventilated area or outdoors.

Spiced Pecans

Set them out and watch them disappear, or box and wrap them as gifts.

1 c. sugar
1 to 2 t. ground cinnamon
1 t. salt
½ t. ground nutmeg
¼ t. ground cloves
¼ c. water
3 c. pecan halves

Combine first six ingredients in a large saucepan. Place over medium heat, stirring constantly until sugar dissolves; then cook to soft ball stage (about 232°). Remove from heat; add pecans, stirring until well coated. Spread pecans on wax paper, and separate nuts with a fork. Cool.

Thyme, Lemon Peel, & Black Pepper Vinegar

Herbal vinegars are visually appealing as well as tasty in salads and as marinades in various dishes. White wine vinegar is delicate in taste and I consider it to be the best in the making of specialty vinegars. For an extra-special touch, I tie ribbons or raffia around the necks of each of my vinegar bottles and label them.

1 large sprig fresh thyme
1 long spiral lemon peel
2 heaping T. black peppercorns
2 c. white wine vinegar

Boil pint-sized resealable containers in water to sterilize (you can use jars, glass soda bottles, or wine bottles with new cork tops). Place herbs in sterilized jars. Add vinegar and seal tightly. Place in light-filled window for one month, giving containers a gentle shake every so often.

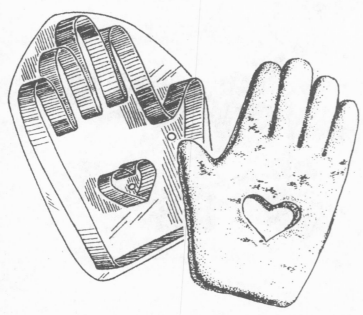

Carrot Chip Cookies

A delicious cousin to the ever-popular carrot loaf.

1½ c. all-purpose flour
1¼ t. ground cinnamon
¾ t. baking soda
½ t. ground nutmeg
½ c. butter
⅓ c. packed light brown sugar
½ c. sugar
1 large egg
¾ c. coarsely grated carrots
½ c. walnuts
⅔ c. white chocolate chips

Preheat oven to 350°. Mix flour, cinnamon, baking soda, and nutmeg. Cream butter, sugars, and egg in a large bowl. With mixer on low speed, blend in carrots, then flour mixture into butter mixture. Beat just until blended. Stir in nuts and chips. Drop by rounded teaspoonsful onto ungreased cookie sheets. Bake 12 to 14 minutes, until edges are lightly browned and crispy. Tops will be soft to the touch. Cool slightly on sheets, then transfer to racks to finish cooling…that is if you can keep everyone from eating them while they are still warm!

Cookie Cutters

A great gift for any child is a basket full of cookie cutters, sprinkles, a child-size apron that you can decorate with the child's name, a rolling pin, and recipes for cut-out cookies and a simple icing. For starters, you could add refrigerated dough found at the supermarket.

Mulling Spice Bags

A gift that brings back a wonderful tradition from Christmases past! Buy a gallon of cider and place in a basket along with the mulling spice. Top with a festive bow.

4 cinnamon sticks
8 whole cloves
8 whole allspice
4 T. grated orange peel

Cut cheesecloth in double thickness into 6" × 4" squares. Place onto each square one cinnamon stick, 2 cloves, 2 allspice, and one tablespoon orange peel. Then bundle up with twine.

Christmas Truffles

These will last up to a month in the refrigerator, unless your family finds them. Then they'll last only a day or two!

⅔ c. heavy cream
12 oz. quality chocolate chips
4 T. unsalted butter, room temperature

Optional (for coating):
cocoa powder
coconut
ground nuts
powdered sugar
chocolate sprinkles

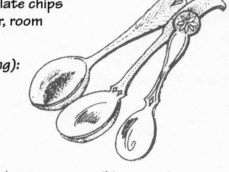

In a heavy saucepan, heat cream until just coming to a boil. Remove from heat and whisk in the chocolate chips and the butter. Beat until smooth. Pour this into a glass dish and place plastic wrap directly on the chocolate mixture. Refrigerate for about three hours. Then, working with clean hands or plastic gloves, take a spoonful of chocolate and roll it between your palms. Dip the ball into cocoa powder, coconut, or other coating, and place in a mini cupcake paper (found in specialty stores just for candy) or on a sheet of wax paper. Place in an airtight container and refrigerate.

"Frost" oranges, lemons, limes, apples, and grapes for holiday garnishes and centerpieces. Simply brush fresh fruit with beaten egg white, then roll in sugar.

My favorite Christmas tradition was celebrating St. Nicholas Day, which falls on December 6. On the night of the 5th, we'd hang our stockings up and go to bed. In the morning, we'd find tangerines, a St. Nick cookie, and a piece of paper. The paper held a rhyme that was a clue to where our gift was hidden. You'd find your gift from St. Nick and tear open the wrapping. I can still "smell" those mornings...the tangerine peel, the nutmeg from the cookie, and the excitement of opening the package. Mom was smart because December 25 seems a lifetime away right after Thanksgiving, so having a little treat earlier helped with the anticipation and excitement of waiting.

St. Nicholas was said to leave gifts, candies, and sweets on window sills, in shoes, and even in stockings of good little children. Hearing of three unmarried daughters without dowries, he left three bags of gold. The daughters were married and the tradition of St. Nicholas began.

We set up our Nativity scene using a small jewelry box for the manger, without the baby Jesus. We place a pile of straw next to it. When the children do good deeds like setting the table, picking up their toys, helping each other, then they get to put a piece of straw in the manger. By Christmas Eve the manger is well padded by good deeds and ready for baby Jesus' arrival on Christmas morning. The children are very proud of the part they play in making his bed comfortable.

One of our favorite family traditions is lining the sidewalk with "luminaires" on Christmas Eve. The candles inside these sand-filled bags are our birthday candles for Jesus. Before our children climb into bed that night, we all go outside and help blow out the "birthday" candles. Doing this has helped teach the children that the real meaning of Christmas isn't the presents or the decorations, but that it's the birth of Christ.

★ ★ ★ ★ ★ ★ ★ ★ ★ ★ ★ ★ ★ ★ ★ ★ ★

My sisters and I like to host our family "Progressive Dinner." Christmas Eve and Christmas Day are very often hectic, busy times, and each of us has her own spouse's families to visit. We decided to set aside a day prior to Christmas, to travel from house to house, visiting. This way the children get to see all the trees decorated and it's a great way to enjoy pre-Christmas festivities, while gearing up for the big day. We each have a suitable dinner course: appetizers at the smallest house so we can mingle, main course at the house with the longest dining table, and desserts at the house where wonderful desserts are made! It works out very nicely and gives us a special day to celebrate the season together.

> **At Christmas play and make good cheer,**
> **For Christmas comes but once a year.**
> **—Thomas Tusser**

FRIENDS

Every Christmas, a group of us ladies gathers at someone's home for a "Christmas Craft Exchange." The craft has to be homemade and we set a cost. We serve Christmas cookies and punch and draw numbers to see who gets what craft. I never would have believed how talented we are. Each year we try to out-do ourselves and always add a few more ladies to the group.

★ ★ ★ ★ ★ ★ ★ ★ ★ ★ ★ ★ ★ ★ ★

Our church has a Christmas workshop for the kids the first Saturday of December. Six or seven crafts are arranged for them to do and they spend about 20 to 30 minutes on each craft. We have a story time first, then do crafts, have lunch, sing carols, and then go back and pick up the last of the crafts. Swags are always made for every family in the congregation. The dads always show up just in time to clean up after the activities!

My husband and I come from large families, and Christmas is spent with many relatives. We decided to make New Year's Eve our special holiday with our seven children. New Year's Eve day is spent preparing snacks and decorating for the festivities. Throughout the evening we play games and enjoy our snacks. At 10 o'clock, we prepare black-eyed peas that are eaten at midnight for good luck in the coming year. When the clock strikes twelve, we have a toast to our family and then each child gives a toast of his or her own. We wind up the evening by shooting off fireworks!

* *

Be sensitive to the needs of our seniors this holiday season. It's not the crystal bud vase or the silk pajamas that they want…it's you. Spend some time together, perhaps a trip to the mall to hear the Christmas music, a ride in the car to enjoy the Christmas lights, services at church, lunch at a favorite restaurant, or give coupons for snow shoveling, grocery shopping, or visits to the doctor. If you live far away and can't be together, a much appreciated gift would be a basket filled with a box of all-occasion cards, a pad of lined paper, stamps, pens, and plain envelopes. Or how about a "big print" book or a magazine subscription? Also, don't forget gift certificates for groceries, long-distance telephone calls, electric or gas service for a month, or a visit to the beauty shop. Remember, a visit and the words, "I love you" can mean more than you would ever imagine!

When traveling with small children, have tiny inexpensive pre-Christmas presents to give them along the way. It helps to keep them occupied. If the children are old enough, give them a map and tell them in which towns or cities they will receive surprises. They'll have fun keeping track.

Each year my father would read from Dickens's *A Christmas Carol* to us in the evenings before going to bed. This would take a full week and the story would end on Christmas Eve.

★ ★ ★ ★ ★ ★ ★ ★ ★ ★ ★ ★ ★ ★ ★ ★ ★

Four years ago I had an idea that has become a Christmas tradition at our house. Throughout the year I purchase small, inexpensive items such as key chains, costume jewelry, little toys, and cassette tapes. Before Christmas, I wrap and tag the boxes and arrange them on a decorated tray. After Christmas dinner, while family and guests linger over dessert and coffee, I sneak upstairs to get the tray of "dessert gifts." It's a nice surprise at the end of the day and helps make the Christmas magic last a little longer.

★ ★ ★ ★ ★ ★ ★ ★ ★ ★ ★ ★ ★ ★ ★ ★ ★

According to the Irish, if you find a bird's nest in your Christmas tree, it is a sign of life and good fortune for the coming year. The first year my husband and I were married we were lucky enough to find such a bird's nest. We've kept it and place it in our tree each year.

Parents with small children, this is for you. When we were growing up my parents bought a new Christmas book for each of us around the middle of November. After the holidays, the books went into a box in the attic. Each year we added to the collection, and I can remember as a child asking my mom to bring down the Christmas box of books as soon as Thanksgiving was over. I kept the collection and added to it when my children were small. Many are tales not found any longer. Our favorite story was "Granny Glittens and Her Amazing Mittens." Each night we would have a story read to us up until Christmas Eve.

I heard a bird sing
In the dark of December
A magical thing
And sweet to remember.
"We are nearer to spring
than we were in September,"
I heard a bird sing
In the Dark of December.
—Oliver Herford

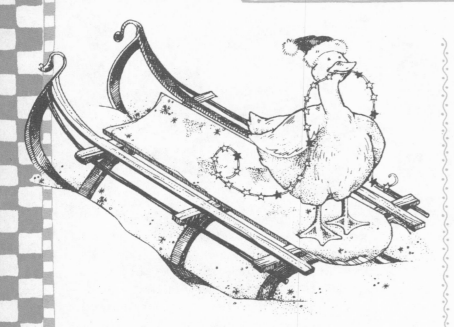

We have a tradition in our family that was started many years ago by my mother, called "Santa's Sleigh." We have a Santa doll and a little wicker sleigh, which sit on a table filled with tiny, but brightly colored, decorated packages. There is one package in the sleigh for each friend and family member who will be sharing Christmas dinner with us. The gifts are not opened until Christmas evening when we are having dessert. Then one of the children gets to pass out a gift to each person. It could be a pair of earrings, a small bottle of cologne, or a toy. The gifts are small, but everyone looks forward to opening them, especially the children, because even after all of the festivities of Christmas Day they know that they will still have one gift left to open.

Start a collection of Christmas books to hand down over the years. Books with Christmas themes, illustrations, stories, poems, recipes… old and new…will be treasured always. You can search new and used bookstores, garage sales, and tag sales. The older books are becoming scarce, but occasionally you can find delightful old Christmas stories. Bring the books out every December to enjoy and share with family.

★ ★ ★ ★ ★ ★ ★ ★ ★ ★ ★ ★ ★ ★ ★

On Christmas Eve, we always pack the kids in our van to go look at Christmas light displays in our city and the suburbs. We have hot cocoa and a special spicy popcorn snack in the car with Christmas carols in the tape deck. Something so simple can be an event if you make it that way.

Long, long ago
Winds through the olive trees
Softly did blow
'Round little Bethlehem
Long, long ago.
Sheep in the hillside lay
Whiter than snow.
Shepherds were watching them
Long, long ago.
Then from the midnight sky
Angels bent low
Singing their songs of joy
Long, long ago.
Soft in a manger bed
Cradled so low
Christ came to Bethlehem
Long, long ago.
—Anonymous

Decorate a tree with cookies! Gnomes, heart in hands, or gingerbread men look great and smell delicious.

Every year, each of my three children selects one old favorite cookie recipe and one new one for us to prepare. It's amazing how favorites change, and how they remember who "discovered" the new favorite.

★ ★ ★ ★ ★ ★ ★ ★ ★ ★ ★ ★ ★ ★ ★ ★ ★

Legend has it that burning a bayberry candle on Christmas Eve brings good luck throughout the New Year.

★ ★ ★ ★ ★ ★ ★ ★ ★ ★ ★ ★ ★ ★ ★ ★ ★

It's been a tradition for my nine grandchildren to come to Grandmother's farm home after Thanksgiving to decorate their own gingerbread houses. I love the holidays and for the children it's a special time. I delight in this quality time with them and as the years go by, the teenagers enjoy this decorating session as much as the little ones. The look on their little faces as they decorate will always be remembered in my heart. And I know that making the gingerbread houses will provide wonderful memories for my grandchildren, who call me "Ava," Portuguese for grandmother.

My daughter's birthday is in December, which gives us a great reason to have a gingerbread house party. I prebake the houses and assemble them ahead of time. When the children arrive, the table is covered with assorted candies to use as decoration. Each child has a bowl of icing with a butter knife and their own house to decorate as they please. No matter how young or old the child, each house turns out beautiful. The houses also become the Christmas centerpieces for their homes for the holidays!

Taking down the Christmas tree is always such a sad experience. I used to hate watching our three boys' sad little faces stare at the barren tree, as it lay on the ground outdoors waiting to be hauled away. Then I had an inspiration! Why not let the boys adorn the tree outdoors for the animals. On the designated day, I give each boy a small jar of peanut butter with a plastic knife, a squeeze bottle of honey, and whatever kind of cereal or crackers we have in the house. We take the tree out and the boys have a ball painting the tree with peanut butter and drizzling it with honey! Then they throw handfuls of cereal or cracker crumbs on the tree, and of course, it sticks to the honey and peanut butter. Once finished, we get hours of enjoyment watching from the windows as an assortment of birds and squirrels come to enjoy our Christmas tree.

★ ★ ★ ★ ★ ★ ★ ★ ★ ★ ★ ★ ★ ★ ★ ★ ★ ★

A favorite tradition that we have passed on to our daughter and her family involves cutting down the Christmas tree each year. We pack either a breakfast or a picnic lunch to have in the woods after we get our tree. How nice it is to have a winter picnic, complete with fire to cook bacon or hot dogs. Yum yum!

Thinking of giving a pet kitten or puppy this Christmas? Be sure it will be wanted and cared for! Include a good book on pet care along with recommended food from your local pet store. Make sure the new "baby" has had its shots. Give it a good start in life with its new owner.

This is a tradition my husband started ten years ago when we got married. He would go to the local greenhouse and buy me a beautiful poinsettia plant. It got to be a little more special when our daughter was born, because then the two of them would go together to buy it. But the best part is when there is a knock at the door and there stands my daughter holding the poinsettia saying, "This is for you, Mommy!" with a big smile on her face and my husband standing behind her with tears in his eyes. I hug them both and my little one always asks, "Why are you crying, Mommy?" and I tell her, "Because I love you and Daddy very much!" I hope this tradition will always continue.

My mother loves almost anything Victorian, and has a collection of demitasse teacups. Believing that we all need to learn to relax and enjoy traditions of another time, she started serving Christmas tea for her grandchildren. They are invited to participate as soon as they are old enough to go to the cupboard and choose their favorite cup for tea time. Each child may pour his or her tea and choose from a selection of tiny sandwiches, petit fours, and cookies. Candles are lit and classical music is played. No matter the age, the grandchildren catch the mood of this special time, and look forward to this tradition for conversation and old-fashioned fellowship during the busy, hectic holidays.

Our children were always asking to open a gift early, so we started our own "Twelve Days of Christmas." In each Christmas stocking go twelve stocking stuffers. We start on December 13th and each morning, before everyone goes their separate ways, we get to open one stocking stuffer. The last one is opened on Christmas Eve. Christmas Day is then left to open all the gifts under the tree.

In our town, we have a "Tree of Life." Some places call it a "Giving Tree." Written on each paper ornament is a description of a needy person and what he or she needs or would like for Christmas. We each choose an ornament with someone about our own age and buy that person a gift, usually something they want, because it makes it a little more special for them. Sometimes, my two boys give an additional item, something they themselves would like to have. Giving a gift to someone, not knowing who is receiving it, gives us a special feeling.

Because the holidays are so busy and the grandchildren seem to receive so many gifts from Santa, my husband and I started a tradition of having the grandchildren open their gifts from us on Christmas Eve. After church, the children come home, settle down with hot chocolate and cookies, and open their special gifts from Gram and Gramps. This way it makes the holidays seem a little longer and more special. It gives the children a chance to realize what Gram and Gramps gave them instead of the gifts being lost in the excitement of Santa's gifts. People on fixed incomes can't afford large gifts, especially when they have several grandchildren, so this special time makes their gifts seem more important and much more fun. When some of the grandchildren live far away, this also makes a special time on Christmas Eve to remember the grandparents who sent the gifts.

For a special mother-daughter memory, take an evening for yourselves right before Christmas. Have a leisurely dinner at a favorite restaurant, exchange little gifts or goodies, then attend a holiday concert. The break from all the hustle and bustle of Christmas will refresh both of you, and spending that very special evening together will become an important part of Christmas every year.

Several years ago on Christmas Eve, my daughter said in fun, "You all should drop by my house in the morning because Bob [my son-in-law] is making breakfast burritos for us." So after they left, we planned an early morning "surprise visit" for my daughter's family. We all went home, looked into our refrigerators, and took any breakfast food to them we could find. It turned out to be a family

tradition to have "Christmas Breakfast Burritos." We gather at different homes on Christmas morning and eat breakfast together. This also gives everyone a chance to join the other sides of their families for an afternoon or evening visit. A lot of families are not the "early morning riser" types that our family is so this gives equal time for everyone.

Have your kids ever asked you how Santa knows if they're naughty or nice? In our house, the answer was easy. The birds know. All year long the birds keep a watch over all the children of the world. We all know that the animals can talk to Santa, so the birds fly to the North Pole and report their findings. Birds can be sitting high in a tree and watching you play in the yard, or they can peek in your window to see if you went to bed on time or did the chores you were told. In our home we always had a bird feeder out the moment the weather turned cold. Remember, the birds are messengers for Santa Claus!

We intentionally extend our tree decorating project to last for days. The first night we all pick out the tree at the nursery. The second night we bring the tree into the house and enjoy the evergreen smell. The third night the lights are put on the tree. The fourth and fifth nights the ornaments are put on the tree by the entire family. Each ornament is taken from its separate sack with its identifying information (where purchased, year, gift from _____, and the like). With each ornament, we reminisce about the people, places, and Christmases past, sharing that history with our son. These evenings are always accompanied by Christmas music.

Recycle your Christmas tree! Some local parks will chip up your Christmas tree, and you can take the chips home and use them for mulch.

One of our family traditions at Christmas is for Santa to leave a jigsaw puzzle (1000 piece) under the tree. This becomes the family "project" for the next few days and helps extend the Christmas holiday, bringing young and old together to help complete the puzzle. It's also been the reason for some late nights for the adults!

The mistletoe bough on the festive throng
Looks down, amid echoes of mirthful song...
And who is she that will not allow
A kiss claimed under the mistletoe bough!
—English Ballad

For those of you with birthdays during the holidays, schedule them for sometime after Christmas so the birthday boy or girl's day doesn't get lost in the shuffle...and you're not faced with another event to plan.

When someone you love becomes a new mother, buy her a large, bound, blank journal and write several family recipes in it. Instruct her to keep adding her child's favorite recipes to the book...favorite cookies, meals, and so forth. Then, the first year that the child has left home, gotten married or moved away, wrap this book up and give it to him or her. Be sure to add the family holiday traditions, and you will give a gift of love that has no price tag. You can also have other close relatives write in a favorite recipe that maybe your child loved during a visit there. Not only will the child have the recipe, but a wonderful sample of "Aunt Linda's" handwriting to remember her by. This is a Christmas present that you cannot buy because it takes years to gather. It's a way of showing how much a child is loved. I have books for both of my children.

We have saved all the Christmas books that my daughters have had since they were little. Each year we put them out in various places around the house for all to enjoy. Each year I also add one or two new books. Children and adults alike enjoy looking at these books, and often they bring back pleasant memories of times past.

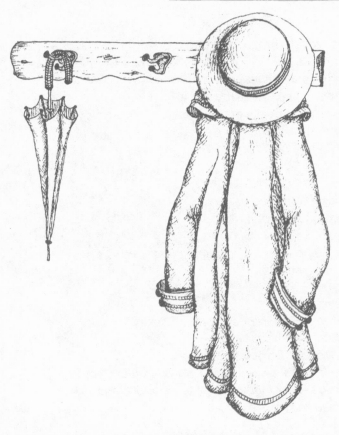

oh-so-hard not to show my disappointment. To my confusion, when the box was opened there was another box inside, all beautifully gift-wrapped and containing…another box. To my child's mind, it seemed those boxes went on forever. With each smaller box hope grew within me, until finally I opened a package with a jewelry box inside. There, on the velvet lining, lay my golden wristwatch.

My dad took the watch from me and showed me something very special. If you held the watch at just the right angle, you could see two tiny diamond chips; one on either side of the watch face. I have had many Christmases since then and have received many wonderful…and much more valuable…gifts than that wristwatch, but in my memory, and for all time, that watch shall remain my "best ever" gift.

★ ★ ★ ★ ★ ★ ★ ★ ★ ★ ★ ★ ★ ★ ★

Picture two little girls in the year 1905, skipping along on their way to school and singing to the first snowflakes of the winter:

Old woman, old woman, old woman up high
She's plucking her geese, see the white
*   feathers fly!*

It was the Christmas of 1941, bleak even for a child because World War II was a mere eighteen days old and no one knew how it would all end. I was eight years old that year and all I wanted for Christmas was a REAL 14-karat gold-filled wristwatch. Christmas Eve arrived. My dad came in the house with lots of packages for my mother, and one gigantic gift-wrapped box for me. I adored my father and I tried so hard to hide my massive disappointment about the size of that box. I wasn't going to get my watch after all. Christmas morning came, and I searched among the packages for a small box addressed to me. Even Santa hadn't left me a small box. My dad passed out the presents, saving the big box until last. When he placed it in front of me, I began to unwrap it, trying

Write a long letter to a friend you haven't seen in a while.

If you would like to keep in touch with family more often than just at Christmas, start a family letter. Make a list of participating family members and their addresses. The first person on the list writes a letter and sends it to the next person on the list. After reading the letter, they add their own and send the two letters on to the next family member on the list. The last person on the list sends all the letters back to the first person on the list. They take out their old letter and insert a new one. One week is a good time to limit for each family to write down their news and get the family letter back in the mail. We keep our old letters in a binder for our own family journal. We also send pictures and good recipes with our family letter.

Traveling through Lancaster, Pennsylvania, this fall, we noticed that many homes had small electric candles glowing in each window. It looked so cheery and welcoming, almost like someone waving hello from inside the house. Now we have also adopted this tradition for harvest and Christmas seasons in our home in California. These candles are relatively inexpensive and not hard to find. Here in southern California we need to keep a candle burning to show a little warmth to our neighbor or to that stranger passing by.

The local garden club sponsors "Christmas Tree Lane," a display of decorated trees by clubs or individuals. It is held on Thanksgiving weekend to inspire the Christmas spirit. This will be my fourth year as a participant and my theme will be "A Jewel of a Tree." Decorations will be handmade and purchased ornaments, earrings and other findings with faux precious stones. Last year my entry was "A Scherenschnitte Tree," which featured hand-cut Christmas ornaments, beeswax hearts and candles (from **Gooseberry Patch**), golden yarrow, and other dried materials.

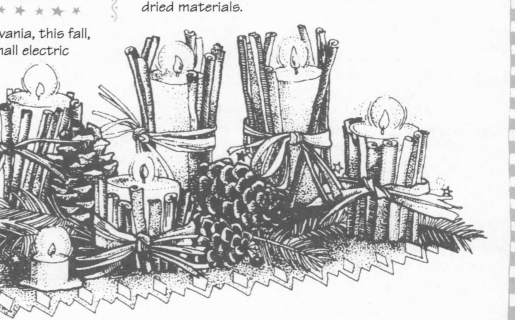

We try to celebrate customs stemming from our ethnic backgrounds. Following Swedish custom, we put a bird's nest in our tree for good luck. I decorate my cookie tree with Swedish gingerbread gnomes. In honor of our German heritage, we celebrate St. Nicholas Day on December 6th, when the children put their shoes out overnight so St. Nicholas can leave them gifts, including the traditional bag of chocolate coins wrapped in gold foil. We also follow the custom of lighting an Advent wreath on the four Sundays before Christmas. We gather greens and pinecones from the woods to make our wreath and then add the four candles. To remember our French ancestors, we serve a bûche de Noël for dessert on Christmas Eve.

★ ★ ★ ★ ★ ★ ★ ★ ★ ★ ★

Celebrate a theme Christmas. For our Williamsburg Christmas, we featured recipes from colonial days such as roast Cornish hen, pecan pie, Yorkshire meat pie, syllabub, and sack posset. The musical background was provided by tapes of colonial-era music. The house was lit entirely by candlelight and featured decorations made with fruit, greens, and nuts. A long swag of pine, studded with lemons and pineapples, made a lovely centerpiece. We also made nut balls and trees by hot gluing nuts and small pinecones to Styrofoam balls and cones. These can be decorated with canella berries or spray painted gold.

"You merry folk, be of good cheer,
For Christmas comes but once a year.
From open door you'll take no harm
By winter if your hearts are warm."
—Geoffrey Smith

One of my most beloved Christmas memories happened a few years ago. After the children were in bed, my husband put on his big work boots and stepped onto a tray filled with talcum powder. He then made footprints on the floor all around the fireplace, the presents, and the cookies and milk, to make it look like Santa had been there. You should have seen my older son's face when he saw those footprints. He knew Santa had really been to his house. With ten years between my two children, my older son will do the footprint honors for his little brother this year.

✶ ✶ ✶ ✶ ✶ ✶ ✶ ✶ ✶ ✶ ✶ ✶ ✶ ✶ ✶ ✶ ✶ ✶ ✶ ✶

Grammy and Grampy moved to Florida and we all missed them so much. We decided to make them a special batch of cookies. We rolled out our favorite sugar cookie dough, then had the kids put their (clean) hands on the dough. We traced their little hands with a plastic knife then baked the cookies. The kids had a great time decorating the cookies, and my parents were absolutely thrilled to get batches of the three different sized hands. My dad even polyurethaned one hand cookie from each grandchild, wrote their name and the date on it and hung them on their tree!

Rather than being on the road Christmas Day, have a family party the Sunday before and ask everyone to bring an appetizer or dessert. You'll enjoy visiting, munching, and exchanging gifts and have a much more relaxing holiday.

Decorating sugar cookies is a family tradition. We set aside one night when everyone, even visitors, joins in. We mainly do gingerbread men, creating everything from football players to self-portraits… all with frosting and lots of imagination.

★ ★ ★ ★ ★ ★ ★ ★ ★ ★ ★ ★ ★ ★ ★

Each Christmas season we have a large (1000 piece) jigsaw puzzle going on a table. Each visitor in and out during the holiday is asked to put at least one piece in and sign their name on a piece of paper. When the puzzle is finished, it's glued to a board, with the signature paper and year glued to the back to keep track of the contributors!

★ ★ ★ ★ ★ ★ ★ ★ ★ ★ ★ ★ ★ ★ ★

Our families and relatives are scattered in different states and across Canada, making Christmas with the relatives difficult. Several days before the holiday, we invite friends to come over for Christmas cheer and tell them to bring the children. Many comment that this is the only time the entire family is invited to an open house. They don't have to find baby-sitters and the kids all have fun with my children.

Christmas Eve is always spent at my parents' home for the traditional Italian "Night of the Seven Fishes." Oysters, shrimp, crab salad, pasta, champagne punch, dessert, and much more. Then, Santa and Mrs. Claus drive through my parents' neighborhood on a fire truck. Believe it or not, this has been a tradition for over 30 years.

Button Cookies

Mix up your favorite cookie dough. Divide dough evenly into four batches, and color each batch with a different food coloring. Roll dough to desired thickness. Using round cutters, cut out a variety of circular cookies. Bake and remove from oven. While cookies are still hot, use a drinking straw to cut four holes in each cookie so cookie resembles a button. Packed in a pretty tin, these treats will resemble Grandma's button box.

We have a family night of decorating cookies. The whole family comes over one evening, on a Saturday, and I bake lots and lots of cookies. When you do this, be sure to take plenty of pictures. The little ones love it!

★ ★ ★ ★ ★ ★ ★ ★ ★

About a week before Christmas, when school is out, we have a cookie decorating party. Both of my children, now 12 and 14, invite three or four friends. Using a butter cookie recipe and lots of different Christmas cookie cutters, we bake about two dozen cookies per person. We also decorate and personalize an apron for each guest. We buy inexpensive, plain aprons. We buy tons of sprinkles, tubes of icing, and colored sparkles. The kids get busy creating, and lots of munching goes on! Milk and hot cider are served, and each guest leaves with a large red or green plastic plate filled with cookies. It's always a hit!

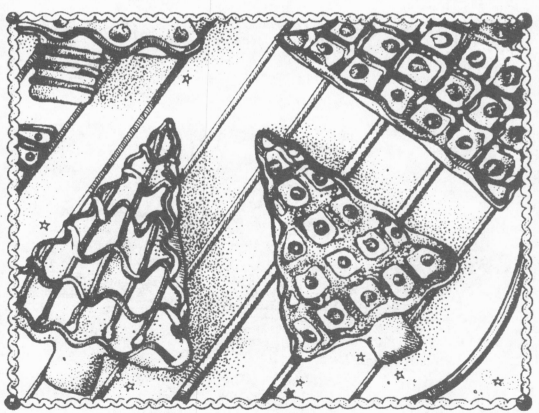

Each member of our family has a candlestick made to hold a very small red candle. We sit before our breakfast plates on Christmas morning, candles lit, while we have a silent moment (well, the kids try) counting our blessings. Then we make our wishes, blow out the candles, and dive into broiled grapefruit and Christmas-bread toast…then we begin emptying our stockings.

One of our favorite traditions is bringing home the tree. For years we've gone to tree farms, carefully selecting and cutting our precious evergreen. Then we "recycle" the tree, at the request of the local lake conservation authority. It places the donated trees in strategic areas of the lake to provide nesting and growing sites for aquatic wildlife. There may be a park or wildlife area in your neighborhood that recycles Christmas trees… it's wonderful to know that your tree can keep on being part of the environment!

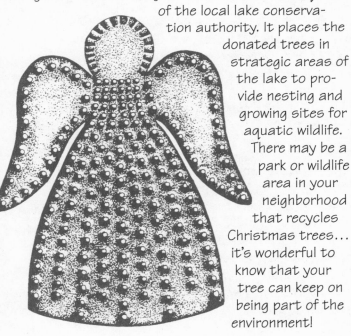

Take time during the holidays to find the homes of shut-ins or live-alones and treat them to carols. If in a rural area, try to arrive in a horse-drawn carriage or sleigh. Afterward, all gather for spice cookies and hot mulled cider.

When older family members, such as grandparents or great aunts and uncles, are visiting for the holidays, keep a guest book handy and ask them to write a page or two of their favorite childhood memories. What was Christmas like at their home? Can they recall their favorite Christmas? Perhaps they could write their favorite recipes in the book for a holiday treat. Your memory book can be packed away each year with the Christmas ornaments and placed out on the coffee table the next year. It's fun to read and recall best memories of those loved ones and their good old days.

Animals have Christmas traditions all their own. So the legend goes, for one hour on Christmas Eve, all animals can speak.

Don a homemade Santa suit and wig and quietly jingle down the halls of a local hospital (get permission first, of course). You'll benefit more than the receivers. The twinkle in your eye won't be mischief, it will be a tear of goodwill.

For the last 30 or more years, my husband and I have always had a small, wrapped gift or favor for each member of the family to open at the Christmas dinner table, before starting the meal. It is a fun, together time, and everyone has a good feeling. It also makes the table look festive.

* * * * * * * * * * * * * * * * * * * *

After the presents are all opened, we sit down and enjoy a big breakfast, often fresh fruit, croissants, and an egg casserole. A small gift box is at each plate, filled with little candies (usually foil-wrapped chocolate coins). A bowl of rice pudding is passed and the one who finds the hidden almond is blessed with good luck! It is then time to go to Grandma's house and celebrate.

* * * * * * * * * * * * * * * * * * * *

Besides buying gifts for friends and family, try to remember those less fortunate. Every year, my husband and I donate food to the community kitchen and pet food to the local animal shelter. Giving of yourself is much more spiritually rewarding than receiving presents.

One of our holiday traditions involves putting candles in all our windows after Thanksgiving dinner. Since we have four floors in our old home and lights in 24 windows, it makes for good exercise to ward off "turkey bloat." Our neighbors always expect the candles, as well as a tree outside, to be lit Thanksgiving evening.

★ ★ ★ ★ ★ ★ ★ ★ ★ ★ ★

This buffet has been a tradition with our family for years. We had six children, so Christmas was a very busy time for us. It didn't take me long to realize that a sit-down meal with these kids was a big mistake. They were so excited and preferred to be playing with their toys. So, I would set up a buffet; when they were hungry, they could help themselves. Most buffet dishes can be made the day before. This gives moms time to enjoy their family. The buffet might include potato salad, baked beans, gelatin fruit salad, meatballs, sliced ham, rolls and bread, and an assortment of Christmas cookies for dessert.

Call your local college or high school to find out names of international students who might like to share a holiday meal and your traditions. They are lonely for family and friends and need to see more of American life than the four walls of a dormitory room.

> The ornament of a house is the
> friends who frequent it.
> —Emerson

Holly lore: The number of berries on a holly plant is said to forecast winter weather. Few berries means a mild winter, as the birds will be able to find food from many sources. An abundance of berries means extra provisions for the birds in view of a harsh winter ahead.

Every year we decorate the house, put up the tree, light the fire in the hearth, make scrumptious food, and invite friends and family over to help decorate the tree. It gives a great feeling of warmth and friendship.

* * * * * * * * * * * * * * * * * *

If there is a church in your community that offers midnight candlelight service, try to attend. When I was a child, my mother, grandmother, aunt, and I would make an event of it. It truly made an impression on me about the true meaning of Christmas. When everyone in the congregation had their candles lit, we would sing "Silent Night." Whenever I hear that hymn, I get a warm feeling in my heart.

Do you know a retired person who might need a little extra income over the holidays? Pay them to bake your cookies, address your cards, wrap your gifts, and save you time. If you're the person with extra time, advertise your holiday services.

One of our family traditions starts a week before Christmas. Our children participate in doing "extra" jobs around the house and in return are paid for doing these tasks. After they have earned enough money, they buy a toy and donate it to "Toys For Tots." We think this helps our children learn that giving to others is what Christmas is all about!

My second son's birthday is November 28th. Traditionally at his party, we plant paperwhites in cups, with white rocks. The kids all take them home as party favors, and by Christmas they have bloomed. So fragrant and fun!

★ ★ ★ ★ ★ ★ ★ ★ ★ ★ ★ ★ ★ ★ ★ ★

I cross-stitch many small ornaments each year, date them and give them to friends and family who look forward to our "ornament of the year."

Host a Christmas workshop. Turn your home into a present-making factory by setting up card tables with rubber stamps, inks, colored pencils, sparkles, scraps of fabrics, ribbon, and paints. Have a fun time making cards, gift wrap, and ornaments.

chapter four **Festive Foods**

Scrumptious Starters

Clam Chowder

A hearty favorite for a cold winter's day!

six ½-oz. cans clams, drained (reserve juice)
1 c. onions, finely chopped
1 c. celery, diced
2 c. potatoes, diced
¾ c. butter
¾ c. flour
1 qt. half-and-half
2 T. red wine vinegar (optional)
1½ t. salt
dash of pepper

Pour clam juice over vegetables in small saucepan. Add enough water to barely cover. Cover and simmer over medium heat until barely tender. In the meantime, melt butter, blend in flour, and cook until smooth and thick. Add half-and-half and stir with wire whip until smooth and thick. Add undrained vegetables, clams, and vinegar. Heat and season to taste.

Corn Chowder

I make this soup with the last picking of corn from the garden, but it's just as good with frozen corn.

1 medium onion, chopped
2 T. butter or margarine
2 c. potatoes, diced
1 c. hot water
2 c. milk
2 T. flour
10-oz. pkg. frozen sweet whole kernel corn
1 t. salt
⅛ t. pepper
parsley

In saucepan, sauté onion in butter, until golden. Add potatoes and hot water. Bring to a boil. Cover, reduce heat, and simmer until potatoes are tender. Gradually stir milk into flour. Add to potatoes along with corn, salt, and pepper. Bring to a boil, reduce heat, stirring occasionally. Simmer about 10 minutes. Garnish with chopped parsley.

Hold a Christmas Eve potluck. Everyone prepares a favorite dish, so one person doesn't get stuck doing all the work!

Easy Velvet Broccoli Soup

Quick and delicious, this is a sure family pleaser.

10-oz. pkg. frozen broccoli, chopped
2½ c. canned uncondensed chicken broth
1 bay leaf
¼ c. onion, chopped
2 egg yolks, beaten
1 t. butter
1 c. light cream or milk
salt and pepper

Bring to a boil in a saucepan broccoli, broth, bay leaf, and onion. Reduce heat, cover, and simmer for 5 minutes or until broccoli is tender. Discard bay leaf. Put soup through a food mill or blender or stir briskly with a wire whisk, for a few seconds. Drop beaten egg yolks and butter into whirling soup. Return to pan, stir in cream, salt, and pepper. Yields 4 servings.

Zucchini Sausage Soup

Very good with warm, crusty bread!

2 lbs. sweet Italian sausage
4 c. celery, diced
4 medium onions, cut into rounds
three 15-oz. cans stewed tomatoes
2 medium zucchini, sliced

Remove sausage from casings. Brown sausage in a deep soup pot. Add celery and onion. Sauté until vegetables are tender. Add tomatoes and zucchini. Let simmer until zucchini is tender. Yields 2 to 3 quarts.

Country Cheese & Cider Spread

These cheese "apples" are fun to make and add flair to any party.

8-oz. pkg. cream cheese, softened
½ c. apple cider
½ lb. Swiss cheese, shredded
½ lb. Cheddar cheese, shredded
½ c. butter, melted
paprika and parsley, for garnish

Beat cream cheese until smooth. Add apple cider, cheeses, and butter. Beat until fluffy. Place this mixture into three buttered cups or containers, mounding tops. Chill overnight. Remove chilled cheese from containers and form each mound into the shape of an apple. Cut stems from real apples and press into each "cheese apple." Coat each cheese apple with paprika. Serve on a parsley-covered plate with crackers and fresh fruit.

Hot Pecan Dip

Hearty flavor and texture in a nutty, toasted appetizer.

½ c. pecans, chopped
2 T. butter, melted
½ t. salt
2 T. milk
2½ oz. dried beef, chopped
¼ c. green pepper, chopped
1 small onion, grated
¼ t. pepper
½ t. garlic powder
½ c. sour cream

Preheat oven to 350°. Mix first three ingredients. Bake for 15 minutes. Remove from oven and set aside. Mix milk, dried beef, green pepper, onion, pepper, and garlic powder. Fold sour cream into mixture. Pour into a 9-inch baking dish (preferably a quiche dish) and sprinkle with the pecan mixture. Bake at 350° for 20 minutes. Serve this hot with party pumpernickel bread or crackers.

Bean Dip

Add a Tex-Mex flavor to your holiday celebrations!

two 10¾ oz. cans chili beef soup
7 oz. chili salsa (medium-hot)
1 small can black olives, sliced
1 lb. Cheddar cheese, grated
1 medium red onion, chopped

Preheat oven to 300°. Mix all ingredients. Bake for 30 minutes. When serving, keep hot in a crock-pot and serve with tortilla chips.

Cheese Sausage Squares

Careful! You might spoil your dinner!

two 15-oz. refrigerated pie crusts
1 lb. pork sausage
2 c. green peppers, chopped
2 c. onion, chopped
two 4½ oz. jars mushrooms, drained
1 t. each: dried basil, garlic powder, dried oregano, crushed red pepper
1 c. Parmesan cheese
16-oz. pkg. American cheese slices
2 c. tomatoes, chopped

Preheat oven to 450°. Unfold and gently roll out both pie crusts. Arrange crusts, slightly overlapping, to cover bottom and side of greased 15" × 10" jelly roll pan. Crimp edges; prick bottom and sides. Bake 10 to 12 minutes. Cook sausage in skillet, add peppers and onions, and sauté until tender. Drain. Stir in mushrooms, seasonings, and ½ cup Parmesan cheese. Place 15 American cheese slices on top, slightly overlapping, to cover crust. Top with filling and remaining cheese slices. Sprinkle with tomato and remaining Parmesan cheese. Bake 10 minutes. Cool 15 minutes. Cut into 1½ inch squares. Yields 5 dozen appetizers.

Rudolph's Nose Herbal Chili Ball

Make ahead of time to allow flavors to blend.

8-oz. pkg. cream cheese, softened
8 oz. sharp Cheddar cheese, grated
2 t. chili powder, divided
½ t. thyme
¼ t. rosemary
1 t. poppy seeds
1 t. sesame seeds
2 t. onion, grated
1 garlic clove, minced
1 t. sherry

Mix cheeses together, add remaining ingredients, and thoroughly beat until smooth. This can be done in a food processor. Refrigerate for 30 minutes, or until the mixture can be handled easily. Shape into a ball or a log.

Roll in chili powder until coated. Wrap in wax paper, then place in a plastic bag. Refrigerate at least 24 hours before serving. Serve with crackers. Yields a one-pound cheese ball or log.

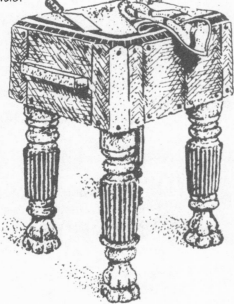

Ham and Swiss Rolls

This recipe was found in a cookbook by Mary Reynolds Smith, and quickly became a favorite at our home many years ago. It's easy to fix, can be made ahead of time and frozen until needed. Another plus, it can be mounded on a platter and surrounded by crackers and crudités. It's a great recipe to have in these hectic times! As an added bonus, you could give a tray of these rolls to a friend and know the happiness of having shared something of yourself…which is, after all, the essence of "giving."

1 lb. baked ham, ground
4 T. Dijon-style mustard
1 medium onion, minced
1 c. butter or margarine, melted
4 oz. Swiss cheese, grated
2 T. poppy seeds
1 T. Worcestershire sauce
4 pkg. (2 doz. each) small finger rolls

Mix first seven ingredients until well blended. Using a serrated knife, slice an entire package of rolls in half, horizontally. Spread the bottom half with ¼ of the ham mixture, replace the top half. Put the rolls back in the foil package, wrap with plastic wrap and then with freezer wrap, and seal tightly. Label and date. Repeat with remaining rolls. When ready to serve, remove from freezer. Preheat oven to 325° and bake rolls for approximately 20 to 30 minutes, until hot throughout.

To use ham mixture as a spread with crackers and fresh vegetables, use only ½ cup butter or margarine and several tablespoons of beef broth, enough to bring it to the proper consistency.

Yuletide Crab Puffs

This recipe can be made ahead of time, adding filling just before serving. Puffs can be frozen for later use.

1 lb. flaked crab meat
⅔ c. celery, chopped
½ c. onion, finely chopped
4 hard-boiled eggs, finely chopped
2 T. chili sauce
salt and pepper to taste
1 T. fresh parsley, minced
1½ to 2 c. mayonnaise

Mix above ingredients together until well blended, adding enough mayonnaise to make the mixture bind together. Refrigerate until shortly before serving. Yields 4 cups of filling.

Puffs:
1 c. water
½ c. butter
1 c. flour, sifted
4 eggs

Bring water to a boil; add butter. Stir until butter is melted. Add flour, stirring until dough forms a ball. Cool dough mixture. Beat eggs in a separate bowl, until very thick and lemon colored. Stir eggs into cooled dough and mix thoroughly. Drop onto a baking sheet by teaspoonfuls. Bake for 15 minutes at 400°. Cool puffs on rack. Slice and fill with crab mixture just before serving. Adding filling too far in advance will result in soggy puffs.

Mushrooms Florentine

Savory and elegant…a big hit!

16-oz. pkg. fresh mushrooms
2 T. butter or margarine, divided
10-oz. pkg. frozen spinach, chopped
¼ to ½ t. garlic powder
½ c. bread crumbs or cracker crumbs
salt and pepper to taste
dash of nutmeg
½ c. Parmesan cheese

Preheat oven to 350°. Wash mushrooms and remove stems. Set stems aside. Melt one tablespoon of butter or margarine. Dip mushroom caps into melted butter or margarine and place cap-side-down into large baking dish. Cook frozen chopped spinach according to package directions. Drain and set aside. Chop mushroom stems and sauté in one tablespoon of melted butter or margarine. Remove from heat. Add spinach, garlic powder, bread crumbs, salt and pepper, nutmeg, and ¼ cup of the Parmesan cheese. Mix well. Fill each mushroom cap with about one tablespoon of spinach mixture. Sprinkle remaining Parmesan cheese on top of filled mushroom caps. Bake for about 20 to 25 minutes. Serve while hot. Yields 10 to 12 servings.

Heap on more wood! The wind is chill;
But let it whistle as it will,
We'll keep our Christmas merry still.
—Scott Marmion

Jalapeño Cornbread

Spice up your New Year's festivities!

½ c. unsalted butter
½ c. onion, chopped
1 clove garlic, minced
1 roasted red pepper, peeled, seeded, and chopped
1 to 2 fresh jalapeños, finely chopped
1 c. whole kernel corn
1½ c. yellow cornmeal
1 c. all-purpose flour
½ c. sugar
1 T. baking powder
1 t. salt
1½ c. buttermilk
2 large eggs, slightly beaten
1 c. Monterey Jack cheese, shredded

Preheat oven to 350°. Melt butter in a 10-inch cast iron skillet. Sauté onion, garlic, red pepper, jalapeños, and corn kernels until tender, about 5 minutes. In a large bowl, sift together cornmeal, flour, sugar, baking powder, and salt. Stir in buttermilk and eggs. Add sautéed mixture, stirring until incorporated. Add cheese and stir. Pour batter back into skillet. Bake for 30 to 35 minutes, until golden brown or when edges are firm to the touch. Let the cornbread sit for 20 to 30 minutes before cutting into wedges.

To roast peppers, place under a broiler until skin is charred, turning as necessary. Place charred peppers in a brown paper bag to steam. When cool, remove skin and seeds. (Do not rinse.)

Eggnog Cherry Muffins

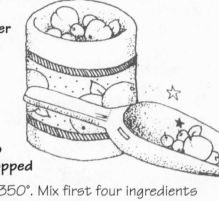

Make an assortment of muffins, including these, and put them out on Christmas morning.

2½ c. all-purpose flour
¾ c. sugar
1 T. baking powder
1 t. salt
1 egg, beaten
1½ c. eggnog
⅓ c. oil
½ c. walnuts, chopped
½ c. maraschino cherries, chopped

Preheat oven to 350°. Mix first four ingredients together. Combine egg, eggnog, and oil, and gently blend into dry ingredients. Stir in walnuts and cherries. Spoon into greased or lined muffin tins and bake for 20 minutes, or until tested done. Yields 12 large muffins.

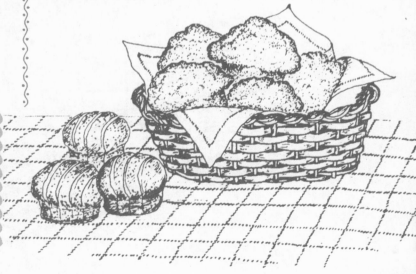

Christmas Crunch Salad

Colorful, festive, and healthy, too!

2 bunches fresh broccoli, broken in small pieces
1 head cauliflower, broken in small pieces
1 red onion, chopped
2 c. cherry tomatoes, cut in halves

Dressing:
1 c. mayonnaise
1 T. vinegar
dash of salt and pepper
½ c. sour cream
2 T. sugar

Combine dressing ingredients, mix well. Toss with vegetables. Serve chilled. Can be made a day ahead, and is particularly pretty if served in a clear glass bowl. Yields 6 servings.

Easy Artichoke Rice Salad

A quick version of a great salad. Try adding ½ cup cooked wild rice to this recipe.

1 pkg. chicken-flavored rice and noodles
2 small jars marinated artichoke hearts, sliced (reserve juice)
1 green pepper, diced
3 celery stalks, diced
1 t. curry powder
½ c. fat-free mayonnaise
12-oz. bottle of green, pimento-stuffed olives, chopped
black pepper to taste

Prepare the rice and noodle mixture according to the instructions on the box. Combine with marinated artichoke hearts and their juice, green pepper, celery, and curry powder. Mix mayonnaise and olives together and blend into rice mixture. Season to taste and chill.

Hearty Holiday Fare

Busy Day Casserole

Easy and satisfying on a cold winter day! A good dish to fall back on around the holidays, when you don't feel like cooking a big meal.

1½ lbs. ground beef or turkey
2 medium onions, chopped
1 large green pepper, cut into thin strips
1 lb. rigatoni, elbow, or shell macaroni
two 15-oz. cans crushed tomatoes
clove of garlic, minced (or ½ t. garlic powder)
black pepper
chili powder to taste
8-oz. block of sharp (or mild) Cheddar cheese, shredded
1 can mushrooms, any size, added to the tomato sauce (optional)

Invite friends over for an address-the-Christmas-cards party. Ask them to bring a snack to share along with their cards, stamps, address books, and return labels. Try to have this event as early in the season as possible. The week after Thanksgiving would be a good time.

In a Dutch oven, brown meat with onions and pepper. Drain off the fat and rinse lightly, then return to pot. Cook the noodles according to package directions, rinse, and set aside. Spray a casserole dish lightly with vegetable spray. Set aside. Put tomatoes in a bowl, add the garlic, a sprinkle of black pepper, and a sprinkle of chili powder, according to taste. In the casserole dish, place enough sauce to cover the bottom. Then add some meat, noodles, more sauce, and half the cheese. Repeat layers, ending with the cheese. Cover with foil and bake at 350° for 45 minutes. Take foil off the last 5 minutes. Serve with rolls and a salad for a quick meal.

This can be made ahead and frozen. Defrost on the counter while you are busy during the day. Pop it in about an hour before dinner. Serves 6 to 8.

Ham 'n Turkey Casserole

Here's what to do with all those leftovers!

3 ribs of celery, chopped
¼ c. butter or margarine
¼ c. flour
½ t. salt
1 c. chicken broth or milk
1 c. light cream
2 T. sherry
3-oz. can mushrooms
2 t. onion, minced (or dried flakes)
2 t. prepared mustard
1 c. sour cream
2 c. cooked noodles (4 oz. dry)
1½ c. cooked turkey, cubed
1½ c. cooked ham, cubed
¼ c. slivered almonds, toasted

Preheat oven to 325°. Sauté the celery in butter until tender yet crispy. Stir in flour and salt. Add broth or milk (broth preferred) and cream. Cook mixture until thick and bubbly, stirring constantly. Stir in sherry, then add remaining ingredients, except almonds. Place mixture in a 2-quart casserole dish and top with almonds. Bake for 25 minutes. May take slightly longer to cook if turkey, ham, and other ingredients are cold when added to the broth and cream mixture. Yields 6 servings.

Enid's Spinach–Cheese Casserole

A classic combination that's always popular.

two 10-oz. pkgs. frozen chopped spinach
10¾-oz. can cream of mushroom soup
2 large eggs, beaten slightly
1 c. mayonnaise
1 c. shredded Cheddar cheese
¼ c. onion, chopped

Preheat oven to 350°. Cook spinach and drain, squeezing out all moisture. Combine with rest of ingredients and turn into large, buttered casserole. Enid and I like one big enough so the casserole isn't thicker than about 2½ inches. Bake for 45 minutes. Yields 12 servings.

Yankee Pleaser Casserole

A one-dish hearty breakfast!

2 lbs. bulk sausage, cooked and drained
2 c. grated cheese (longhorn, Cheddar, whatever you like)
4 eggs
1 c. cooked grits
8½-oz. pkg. corn muffin mix
1¾ c. hot milk
½ c. butter, melted

Preheat oven to 350°. Grease a 2-quart casserole dish. Layer the sausage and one cup of cheese in bottom of casserole. In medium bowl, combine the eggs, grits, muffin mix, milk, and butter. Pour over the sausage and cheese. Top with remaining cheese. At this point, the uncooked mixture may be refrigerated overnight, if desired. Bake for one hour in the middle of the oven. Yields 8 to 10 servings.

Christmas Meatloaf

Super simple! Make this during that hectic week of Christmas. Put it together the night before a very busy day, then all you have to do is pop it in the oven.

1 lb. ground beef
1 c. Italian bread crumbs
1 egg
2 T. onion, minced
¼ c. celery, chopped
¼ c. carrot, grated
¼ c. green pepper, chopped
8-oz. can Italian stewed tomatoes, drained
1 t. dry mustard
½ t. oregano
½ t. salt
½ t. black pepper

Preheat oven to 350°. Combine all ingredients and place in a greased 9-inch loaf pan. Bake for one hour.

Stromboli

Adds an Italian flair to your holiday table!

16-oz. loaf of frozen bread dough, thawed
1 c. (4 oz.) mozzarella cheese, shredded
¼ lb. pepperoni, sliced
3 oz. sliced provolone cheese
¼ lb. thinly sliced ham
1 T. melted butter or margarine
pizza sauce

Preheat oven to 375°. Place bread dough on a lightly greased baking sheet. Pat to a 15" × 10" rectangle. Arrange mozzarella cheese lengthwise down center; layer with pepperoni, then provolone, and ham last. Moisten edges of dough with water. Bring each long edge of dough to center; press edges together securely to seal ends. Brush loaf with melted butter, and bake for 20 minutes or until lightly browned. Cool on wire rack. Electric knife works best for slicing. Offer pizza sauce alongside for dipping. Yields approximately 12 slices.

**This is the week
when Christmas comes.
Let every pudding
burst with plums,
And every tree bear
dolls and drums,
In the week when
Christmas comes.
—Eleanor Farjeon**

Chicken Breasts with Champagne Sauce

Elegant, delicious, and, best of all…it's easy!

2 T. margarine
4 boneless chicken breasts
½ c. fresh mushrooms
⅓ c. champagne
⅓ c. sour cream

Preheat oven to 350°. Heat margarine in saucepan and add chicken. Brown on both sides. Remove chicken to a baking dish. Sauté mushrooms and set aside. Stir champagne into drippings. Simmer until well heated. Pour over chicken, cover and bake for 20 minutes. Remove chicken to platter, reserve liquid. Add sour cream and salt and pepper, to taste, to the reserved liquid. Whisk until smooth. Pour over chicken and top with mushrooms. Yields 4 servings.

BREAD FRESH BAKED

Orange Chicken

Just as delicious with the skin removed. Try this one with brown rice, too!

2½- or 3-lb. pkg. select chicken pieces
   (breasts, thighs, and drumsticks)
salt and pepper
medium white onion, sliced
1 c. orange juice
⅓ c. honey
1 T. soy sauce
2 T. flour
2½ c. cooked white rice

Preheat oven to 325°. Wash and dry chicken pieces, seasoning with salt and pepper as desired. Make a bed of sliced onions in a large baking pan. Lay chicken pieces on onions. Whisk together orange juice, honey and soy sauce. Pour over chicken and bake for one hour or until done. Remove chicken and place pan on stove burner. Add flour and cook until sauce is slightly thickened. Serve over white rice.

Cranberry–Orange Glazed Cornish Hens

This makes a wonderfully delicious holiday dinner for two.

2 fresh or frozen Rock Cornish game hens
2 T. butter, melted
salt and pepper

Sauce:
¼ c. whole cranberry sauce
2 T. orange marmalade
1 T. lemon juice
1 t. minced dried onion
1 t. cornstarch
½ c. mandarin orange sections, drained

Thaw hens, if frozen. Rinse hens and pat dry. Coat inside and outside of hens with melted butter; sprinkle with salt and pepper. Place hens, breast side up, on a rack in a shallow roasting pan. Insert a meat thermometer. Cover loosely with foil. Roast in 375° oven for 30 minutes. Uncover and roast about one hour more or until meat thermometer registers 185°. Meanwhile, make sauce by combining cranberry sauce, marmalade, lemon juice, onion, and cornstarch in a one-quart saucepan. Cook and stir until thick and bubbly. Cook 2 more minutes, stirring constantly. Remove from heat; stir in orange sections. Brush over hens several times during last 20 minutes of roasting.

Chicken Breasts Chablis

Delicious and tender. Add mushrooms to the sauce, if you like.

¼ c. flour
1 t. salt
¼ t. pepper
4 large chicken breasts (boneless and skinless)
5 T. butter
2 T. olive oil
2 T. cornstarch
1 T. Dijon mustard
1½ c. milk
1 t. salt
¾ c. Chablis or other white wine
¼ t. tarragon

Preheat oven to 350°. Mix flour, salt, and pepper. Dredge chicken in flour mixture and sauté in 2 tablespoons of butter and olive oil until brown. Arrange in baking dish. To make the sauce, melt 3 tablespoons butter in a saucepan. Whisk in cornstarch and mustard. Cook until it comes to a boil (keep whisking) and add milk, salt, wine, and tarragon. Cook until it thickens, stirring constantly. Cook one minute, then pour over chicken. Cover and bake 45 minutes to an hour. Serve over hot cooked noodles, rice, or mashed potatoes.

Chicken Divine

This one is truly heavenly!

one 20-oz. bag frozen broccoli
four 5-oz. cans chicken breast or 5 to 6
    cooked boneless chicken breasts
2 cans cream of chicken soup
8 to 10 oz. mayonnaise
curry powder (mild or hot)
3 c. shredded Cheddar cheese
margarine
1½ c. cornflake crumbs

Cook broccoli according to package directions and place in the bottom of a 15" × 9" glass casserole dish. Place chicken on top of the broccoli. In a mixing bowl combine soup, mayonnaise, and curry powder (to taste). Spread mixture on top of chicken and broccoli. Layer top with shredded cheese. Melt margarine (enough to moisten cornflake crumbs when added). Combine crumbs and butter. Spread on top of the casserole. Place in 350° oven and bake for 45 minutes or until cornflake crumbs brown slightly. Remove from oven and serve. Yields 6 to 8 generous servings.

Ring out the old, ring in the new,
Ring happy bells, across the snow;
The year is going, let him go;
Ring out the false, ring in the true.
—Alfred Lord Tennyson

Vegetable Chili

Always welcome on a cold day, this chili is guaranteed to warm up the whole family…and it's healthy, too!

¾ c. olive oil
1 medium eggplant, cut in small cubes
2 medium yellow onion, diced
2 large bell peppers, diced
4 cloves garlic, finely chopped
two 35-oz. cans plum tomatoes
2 T. chili powder
1 T. ground cumin
1 T. dried oregano
1 T. dried basil
2 t. freshly ground black pepper
1 t. salt
1 t. fennel seed
½ c. fresh parsley, chopped
1 can dark red kidney beans, drained
1 can chick peas, drained
½ c. fresh dill (dried will also do)
2 T. fresh lemon juice
1 T. coarse or kosher salt

In a large skillet, over medium heat, sauté eggplant in ½ cup of olive oil until tender. Pour softened eggplant into crock pot or large soup pan. In same skillet, sauté remaining oil, onion, green pepper, and garlic until softened. Add to eggplant mixture in crock pot or Dutch oven. Slowly stir in, over low heat, tomatoes (crushed with hands), chili powder, cumin, oregano, basil, black pepper, salt, fennel seed, and chopped parsley.

Cook uncovered for at least 30 minutes. Can cook up to several hours depending on how well you like to simmer the vegetables and how thick you like your chili. Stir in beans, dill, and lemon juice. Stir to taste and adjust seasoning according to taste. Serve with brown rice and shredded Cheddar cheese for a warm and wonderful holiday meal!

Shrimp Scampi

Christmas dinner doesn't have to be the traditional turkey meal…especially for shrimp lovers!

4 T. butter
2 T. virgin olive oil
2 T. vegetable oil
2 T. fresh parsley, snipped
4 T. fresh lemon juice
2 lbs. jumbo shrimp, fresh or frozen, peeled, deveined, and butterflied

Preheat oven to 450°. Put butter in a 13" × 9" baking dish. Place in preheated oven and heat until butter is foamy. Remove from oven. Add the oils, parsley, and lemon juice to the butter and stir. Add shrimp, turning to coat with butter mixture. Arrange shrimp. Bake 6 to 10 minutes depending on the size of the shrimp. Remove from oven and serve immediately. This goes well with rice, a green salad, and broccoli with cheese sauce.

Christmas Luncheon Crabmeat Bisque

To make a shrimp bisque, replace crab with 1½ cups cooked, peeled, deveined shrimp.

6 T. butter or margarine
4 T. green pepper, finely chopped
4 T. onion, finely chopped
1 scallion, chopped
2 T. parsley, chopped
1½ c. fresh mushrooms, sliced
2 T. flour
1 c. milk
1 t. salt
⅛ t. white pepper
dash of hot pepper sauce
1½ c. half-and-half
1½ c. cooked crabmeat (canned or fresh)
3 T. dry sherry

Heat 4 tablespoons butter or margarine in a skillet. Add green pepper, onion, scallion, parsley, and mushrooms, and sauté until soft, about 5 minutes. In saucepan, heat remaining margarine or butter and stir in flour. Add milk and cook, stirring until thickened and smooth. Stir in salt, pepper, and hot pepper sauce. Add sautéed vegetables and half-and-half. Bring to a boil, stirring. Reduce heat. Add crabmeat, simmer uncovered for 5 minutes. Stir in sherry just prior to serving. Yields 4 servings.

Easy Cheese~ Scalloped Potatoes

A great crowd pleaser!

8 c. potatoes, thinly sliced
3 c. flour
8 oz. colby cheese, shredded
1 medium onion, chopped
½ red pepper, chopped
½ green pepper, chopped
6 slices bacon, fried crisp
6 T. butter
3 c. milk or cream
2½ t. salt
½ t. paprika
½ t. mustard

Preheat oven to 350°. Grease a large casserole baking dish. Shake potato slices in a bag with flour. Place potatoes, cheese, onions, pepper, and crumbled bacon in casserole in four layers, and dot with butter. Heat milk, salt, paprika, and mustard until hot and pour mixture evenly over the potatoes. Bake for 1½ hours, covering for the first half hour. Yields 10 servings.

Holiday garlands for your mantel or table are easy to make. Using florist's wire, attach lady's apples, tangerines, lemons, and limes to a pine garland, weaving French wire ribbon in and out amongst the greenery. For an old-fashioned look, string cranberries on wire and weave throughout your garland.

Hang the merry garlands over all the town.
Smell the spicy odors of cookies turning brown!
The mice have come to nibble,
they're feeling mighty gay—
But only little children shall
have my sweets today!
—Anonymous

Beef Hash

Hearty and filling, just right for an old-fashioned holiday brunch.

1 T. butter
½ c. onion, coarsely chopped
½ c. green pepper, coarsely chopped
2 c. potatoes, peeled, diced
¾ lb. cooked roast beef, diced into ½-inch pieces
14½-oz. can diced tomatoes
1 garlic clove, minced
½ t. pepper

Melt butter over medium heat in a large skillet. Add onion and green pepper; sauté for 3 minutes. Add remaining ingredients and cook until potatoes are tender (about 25 minutes), stirring frequently. Season to taste with salt. Yields 2 large servings.

Corned Beef & Cabbage

Very tasty...try this recipe in your slow cooker and let it simmer all day.

2 lbs. corned beef brisket
½ c. onion, diced
1 bay leaf
1 head of cabbage, cut into wedges
1 lb. of carrots, diced

Place all ingredients in a Dutch oven. Cover brisket with water, bring to a slow boil; then reduce heat and simmer over low heat for 2 hours. Remove bay leaf.

> Laugh and be merry together, like brothers akin,
> Guesting awhile in the room of a beautiful inn.
> Glad till the dancing stops,
> and the lilt of the music ends.
> Laugh till the game is played;
> and be you merry my friends.
> —John Masefield

Roast in Sherry

The wonderful flavor of this roast will make it a family favorite...and the chef's favorite, too, since it's so easy!

5 or 6 lb. chuck roast
1 pkg. dry Italian salad dressing mix
1 lb. fresh mushrooms, sliced
1 large onion, sliced
1 can beef consommé
3 c. cream sherry

Make deep cuts on top of beef. Rub with dry salad dressing mix. Stuff slits with mushrooms and onions. Pile what is left on top of roast. Combine sherry and beef consommé. Pour over top of roast. Cover and let set overnight. Preheat oven to 400°. Bake for one hour; turn heat down to 250°, and bake 4 to 5 hours. Serve with oven-roasted potatoes.

Christmas Breakfast Strata

A great Christmas breakfast. This can be made late Christmas Eve and popped in the oven on Christmas morning.

1 loaf French bread, sliced, buttered, and torn into pieces
2 c. Cheddar cheese, shredded
2 c. Monterey Jack cheese, shredded
2 rolls breakfast sausage, cooked
1 can green chilies, diced
1 small can black olives, sliced
8 oz. mushrooms, sliced
6 to 8 large eggs
4 c. milk
2 T. oregano
1 t. salt
1 t. dry mustard
1 t. powdered onion

Preheat oven to 350°. Butter 13" × 9" and 8" × 8" baking pans and place bread pieces in the bottom of the pans. Sprinkle cheeses over the bread. Sprinkle the cooked sausage, diced green chilies, olives, and mushrooms over the cheese. Beat the eggs and add milk, oregano, salt, dry mustard, and powdered onion. Pour liquid over the sausage mixture and sprinkle with any remaining cheese. Bake for one hour or until a knife blade comes out clean. Serve with sour cream and salsa. Serve English muffins and fresh fruit alongside.

Christmas is the time to bring out your favorite embroidered linens, bedding, and table dressings.

Mel's Christmas Morning Casserole

A whole breakfast, baked and ready to go!

6 eggs, slightly beaten
½ c. Cheddar cheese, shredded
½ c. mozzarella cheese, shredded
1 t. dry mustard
1 T. parsley flakes
1 T. dried onion flakes
1 t. oregano
1 lb. ground Italian sausage, browned and drained
1 c. biscuit mix
2 c. milk

On Christmas Eve, mix all ingredients and pour into a lightly greased lasagna pan. Cover and refrigerate overnight. On Christmas morning, while everyone is opening gifts, pop the pan into a 350° oven and bake for one hour. Yields 10 to 12 servings.

Note: to save fat, sodium, and calories, you can substitute fat-free egg substitute for eggs, low-fat biscuit mix for regular, omit up to ¼ cup cheese, substitute low-fat skim or 2-percent milk, and rinse cooked Italian sausage in hot water, draining well before adding.

Overnight Egg Omelet

Make it the night before and you can relax the next morning.

6-oz. box plain croutons
2 c. sharp Cheddar cheese, grated
8 eggs
1 t. salt
1 t. prepared mustard
dash of pepper
4 c. milk
crisp crumbled bacon

The evening before, grease a 13" × 9" baking pan. Layer croutons, then cheese in the pan. In a bowl, combine eggs, salt, mustard, pepper, and milk. Whip with wire whisk and pour over croutons and cheese. Sprinkle bacon on top. Cover and refrigerate overnight. The next morning, bake for 55 minutes at 325°, or until set. Cut into serving pieces. Serves 8 to 10.

Warm Country Gingerbread Waffles

Can be served with brown sugar, powdered sugar, hot maple syrup, or berries.

2 c. flour
½ t. salt
½ t. ground ginger
1 t. cinnamon
1 c. molasses
½ c. butter
1½ t. baking soda
1 c. cream or sour milk
1 egg

Sift first four ingredients. Heat molasses and butter until butter melts. Remove from heat and beat in baking soda. Add milk and egg, then add sifted flour mixture. Bake batter in waffle iron, making sure that iron is not too hot. Yields 6 to 8 waffles.

Delectable Sweets

Christmas Cranberry Roll-Up Cookies

The red color of these cookies makes them very pretty for the holidays. They are not difficult to make, and it's easy to prepare the dough ahead of time.

2 c. fresh cranberries
1 c. sugar
1 t. orange peel
¼ c. finely chopped almonds
2 c. all-purpose flour
¼ t. salt
1½ t. cardamom
½ c. unsalted butter
1 large egg
1 t. vanilla

In a saucepan combine the cranberries, ¼ cup sugar, and orange peel. Add enough water to partially cover. Cook about 15 minutes, or until berries pop and most of water has evaporated. Cool mixture. Combine flour, salt, and cardamom. In a separate bowl, cream butter, ¾ cup sugar, egg, and vanilla. Add flour mixture. Divide dough in half. Chill. Roll both halves into 12" × 7" rectangles on waxed paper. Spread cranberries and almonds over each rectangle. Roll up like a jelly roll, wrap in plastic wrap and chill for at least 2 hours (at this point it can be frozen). Slice rolls into ¼-inch slices and bake one inch apart on lightly greased cookie sheet at 400° for 12 minutes. Cool completely.

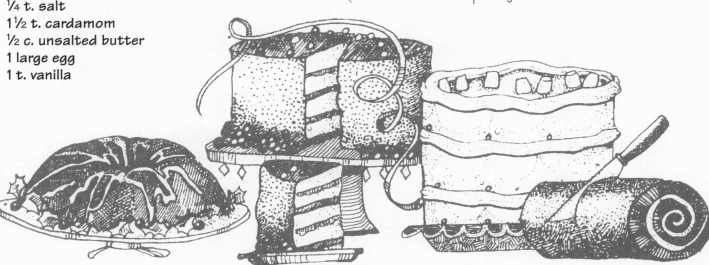

Grandma's Apple Crisp

Serve warm with vanilla ice cream. Yummy!

8 to 10 apples, peeled, cored, and sliced
1 3/4 c. sugar, divided
1 T. cinnamon
nuts (optional)
1 c. all-purpose flour
1/4 t. salt
1 t. baking powder
1 egg
6 T. butter

Preheat oven to 350°. Fill a large glass 13" × 9" × 2" baking dish three-fourths full of sliced apples. Top with 3/4 cup sugar and cinnamon, adding nuts if desired. Let stand while you mix together the flour, one cup sugar, salt, and baking powder. In a separate bowl, beat egg until light, and work into flour mixture until crumbly. Place crumble mixture over apples. Melt butter and pour over the top. Bake for 45 minutes, until crust is lightly browned. Yields 16 servings.

Lemon Snowdrops

Tart and sweet, a perfect combination!

1 c. butter
1/2 c. powdered sugar
1 t. lemon extract
2 c. flour
1/4 t. salt

Filling:
1 egg, slightly beaten
grated rind of 1 lemon
2/3 c. granulated sugar
3 T. lemon juice
1 1/2 T. butter, softened

Preheat oven to 350°. Cream together butter and powdered sugar, add lemon extract. Sift flour and salt together; add to creamed mixture, mixing well. Using level teaspoons of dough, form balls. Flatten slightly. Place one inch apart on ungreased baking sheet. Bake for 8 to 10 minutes. Let cool. Make lemon butter filling by combining beaten egg, rind, granulated sugar, lemon juice, and butter in top of double boiler. Cook over hot water until thick, stirring constantly. Let cool. Put 2 cookies together with filling between. Roll in powdered sugar. Yields 2 1/2 to 3 dozen.

Peanut Butter Cookies with Icing

For this recipe I use chocolate icing the most, simply because it is everyone's favorite. However, I have changed the icing to butter cream or plain white with different food colorings for the occasion. For Christmas, for example, use the white icing with red food coloring for the top and cinnamon candy. The combinations are endless, and the kids will love them.

½ c. shortening (butter-flavored is great)
½ c. smooth peanut butter
½ c. granulated sugar
½ c. light brown sugar
1 large egg
½ t. vanilla
2 c. plus 2 T. all-purpose flour
½ t. baking soda
½ t. salt

Preheat oven to 350°. Cream shortening with peanut butter and both sugars. Add egg and vanilla and beat until light and fluffy. Sift flour, baking soda, and salt over creamed mixture and blend together completely. Form into one-inch balls. Place on a greased baking sheet. Press flat with a fork crossways. Bake for 12 to 15 minutes. Yields 3 dozen.

Pile cookie cutters into an old wooden or depression glass bowl or basket. Display for an instant antique decoration. Accent with greenery for the holidays.

Icing:
1 c. semisweet or milk chocolate morsels
½ t. shortening or vegetable oil
1 c. chopped pecans or cashews, optional

Melt together chocolate morsels and oil on top of double boiler. Stir until blended and smooth but do not allow to boil. Or place in a microwave-safe dish and melt for one minute on high; stir until smooth. Place one teaspoon of melted chocolate on the cooled cookies where the fork made an indentation and spread around. Sprinkle a few chopped nuts on top, if desired. When completely cooled and chocolate has hardened, place in an airtight container.

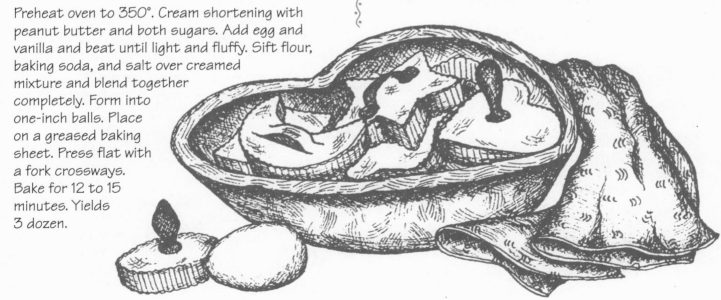

Rudolph Cookies

For Rudolph cookies, mix up a batch of your favorite sugar cookies or gingerbread cookies. Roll out and cut out gingerbread men. Bake as directed in your recipe, and cool. Turn the cookie upside down as if he is standing on his head. The head will be the head for Rudolph, while the arms will be his ears and legs will be his antlers. Use frosting to make the eyes and a big red nose. Decorate the antlers with lines of white icing. Place two green holly leaves above the eyes and a red bow on top to finish him off for the holiday. These cookies are fun for the kids to make. You could use a round jellied candy for the nose. Be creative!

Stained-Glass Cookies

Here's how to make beautiful stained-glass cookies. Using sugar cookie dough, roll out to a ¼-inch thickness on a slightly floured board. With cookie cutters, cut dough into desired shapes. Cut a smaller version of cookie shape on each cookie, leaving a ½- to ¾-inch border of dough. Cut out and remove dough in center of cookies (to save time, and avoid tracing, use a smaller version cookie cutter to cut out the center). Place on baking sheets lined with foil. Then take five rolls of crushed Life Savers or Life Saver holes and spoon candy into the center of the cookies. Bake until candy is melted and cookie is slightly brown. Cool completely before removing from pan.

Crispy Oatmeal Cookies

An old-time favorite, these oatmeal cookies may become a family tradition.

1 c. butter or margarine, softened
1 c. sugar
1 c. brown sugar, lightly packed
2 eggs
2 t. vanilla
1½ c. flour
1 t. baking powder
1 t. baking soda
2 c. oatmeal
2 c. crispy rice cereal
1 c. coconut

Preheat oven to 350°. Cream the butter and sugars. Add eggs and vanilla. Sift the flour, baking powder, and baking soda; add to egg mixture. Add remaining ingredients and mix well. Drop by heaping teaspoonful 2 inches apart on a greased baking sheet. Bake for 10 minutes. Remove from baking sheet at once. Yields 5 to 6 dozen.

Coconut Meringue Cookies

My kids call these "magic cookies."

1 box angel food cake mix
½ c. water
1 t. vanilla
2 c. coconut

Preheat oven to 350°. Whip egg white packet with water and vanilla until stiff. Fold in dry ingredients packet and coconut. Line cookie sheets with tin foil. Drop by teaspoonsful 2 inches apart on cookie sheet. Bake for 12 minutes. Remove cookies from foil when completely cooled. Yields 4 to 5 dozen.

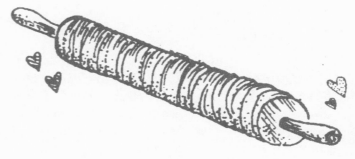

I Love Shortbread

Everyone loves shortbread, buttery and delicious!

¾ c. butter, softened (margarine not recommended)
¼ c. sugar
1¾ c. all-purpose flour
dash of salt
powdered sugar

Preheat oven to 350°. Cream together butter and sugar. Stir in flour and salt. Mixture will be dry and crumbly. With clean hands, pinch mixture until it all sticks together. Shape dough into a ball. Sprinkle clean work surface with flour. Place dough on surface and roll out to a ¼-inch thickness. Cut out with favorite cookie cutters. Place 2½ inches apart on cookie sheet and bake until golden brown on edges (about 10 to 15 minutes). Place powdered sugar into a shaker and dust over each cookie to lightly cover.

Invite a dozen friends over for a cookie exchange and have them each bring 3 dozen cookies packaged in threes. Each guest will go home with 3 dozen cookies (12 different kinds). Share recipes and have a great time!

Maple Nut Cookies

My best friend Ann, now 71, walks from her house down the mountain up to my place every day. She always brings flowers…glorious big blossoms from her garden, and when these are not abundant, she brings cookies. I gave her this recipe and she has added our local, delicious, fresh-picked elderberries to it. Sometimes a batch may come with dried cranberries baked in instead. Ah, the most delicious sort of friendship!

½ c. butter
¾ c. maple syrup
2 c. whole wheat pastry flour
½ t. salt
½ t. baking powder
1 t. vanilla
pecan meats

Preheat oven to 325°.
Mix all ingredients together.
Roll dough into balls.
Flatten out and put a pecan in the middle. Bake about 7 to 10 minutes.

When planning to bake cookies, I couldn't be more organized than with my country cookie cutter basket. My basket includes cookie basics such as cutters and recipes. And decorating the basket when not in use is as much fun as baking!

Banny's Southern Cream Cookies

Five generations of women in our family have made these cookies. It's my great-grandmother's recipe (Ol' Banny, as we called her). The cookies were originally made with black walnuts because that is what Banny had, but you can substitute English walnuts or pecans with equally good results. Of course, that statement has led to many heated discussions, with each nut having its loyal following.

1 c. shortening
2 c. plus 3 T. sugar
3 beaten eggs
1 t. vanilla
1 c. sour cream
5 c. flour
1 t. salt
3 t. baking powder
½ t. baking soda
1½ c. chopped, black walnuts
1 t. cinnamon

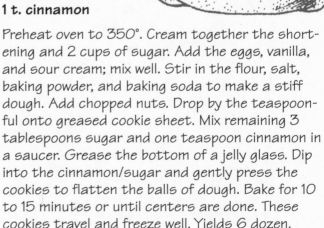

Preheat oven to 350°. Cream together the shortening and 2 cups of sugar. Add the eggs, vanilla, and sour cream; mix well. Stir in the flour, salt, baking powder, and baking soda to make a stiff dough. Add chopped nuts. Drop by the teaspoonful onto greased cookie sheet. Mix remaining 3 tablespoons sugar and one teaspoon cinnamon in a saucer. Grease the bottom of a jelly glass. Dip into the cinnamon/sugar and gently press the cookies to flatten the balls of dough. Bake for 10 to 15 minutes or until centers are done. These cookies travel and freeze well. Yields 6 dozen.

Gingerbread Cookies

It's just not Christmas without gingerbread.

1 c. brown sugar
1 c. light molasses
1 c. shortening (not oil), melted
1 egg, beaten
1 t. ginger
pinch of salt
1 t. cinnamon
½ c. hot water
1 T. baking soda
5 c. all-purpose
   flour

Mix together sugar, molasses, melted shortening, egg, ginger, salt, cinnamon, hot water, and baking soda. Add flour to make a soft dough. Chill for one to two hours. Roll out and cut with gingerbread boy cookie cutter (from **Gooseberry Patch**, of course). Sprinkle on granulated sugar before baking. Bake in 350° oven for 10 to 12 minutes. Yields 3 to 4 dozen cookies, but it really depends on size of cutter and how thick you make the cookies (the thicker cookie is softer).

Farmhouse Chocolate Mint Cookies

These cookies are great if you love mint-chocolate, and they're always a hit at the annual Christmas cookie exchange.

¾ c. butter
1½ c. light brown sugar, firmly packed
2 T. water
12-oz. pkg. semisweet chocolate pieces
2 eggs
2½ c. flour
1¼ t. baking soda
½ t. salt
1 lb. green chocolate mint wafer candies
chocolate sprinkles

Place butter, sugar, and water in saucepan on low heat until butter is melted. Add chocolate pieces and stir until partially melted. Remove from heat. Continue to stir until chocolate is completely melted. Pour into a large mixing bowl and let stand about 10 minutes to cool slightly. With mixer at high speed, beat in eggs one at a time. Reduce speed to low and add combined flour, baking soda, and salt, beating just until blended. Chill dough about one hour. Heat oven to 350°. Line 2 cookie sheets with foil. Take tea-spoonsful of dough and roll into balls. Place two inches apart on cookie sheets. Bake 11 to 13 minutes (do not overbake). Immediately place mints on hot cookie. Allow to soften, then swirl mint over cookies and decorate with chocolate sprinkles. Remove from cookie sheet and cool completely.

Frosted Party Cookies

My love for cookies (always homemade, never store-bought) stems from my grandmother's unsurpassed cookie baking. Each Christmas we would receive in the mail a plain white corrugated box. The cookies within were a sight to behold. There were sugar cookies of every shape, sprinkled with colored sugar or painted to perfection with satiny icing. Each box contained two Santa heads. The faces were painted with food coloring and the beard and fur on his cap were shredded coconut… much too beautiful to eat! Grandmother made little date bars rolled in powdered sugar and a variation of the Thumbprint Cookie she called "Party Cookies." What warm memories this talented lady created for everyone who received a big box of her cookies.

Cookies:
½ lb. butter, room temperature
5 T. powdered sugar
2 c. all-purpose flour
½ t. vanilla
1 c. nuts, ground into flour (pecans are best)
1 t. water

Combine ingredients. Chill in refrigerator for at least ½ hour. Roll into small balls (¾ to 1 inch in diameter). Press lightly with thumb. Place on lightly greased cookie sheets and bake in preheated 350° oven for 10 minutes or until light brown. Remove to rack to cool. Frost. Yields about 30 cookies.

Frosting:
1 c. powdered sugar
3 T. shortening
3 T. meringue powder
6 T. warm water

Combine ingredients. If frosting is too thin, add more powdered sugar. Tint with desired color or leave white.

Orange Iced Cranberry Cookies

Make these for Thanksgiving or Christmas... they're a sure-fire holiday hit.

¾ c. sugar
½ c. brown sugar
½ c. margarine or butter, softened
½ c. sour cream
1 t. vanilla
2 eggs
2¼ c. all-purpose flour
½ t. baking soda
½ t. baking powder
1 c. fresh cranberries, chopped
½ c. walnuts, chopped

Preheat oven to 350°. In a large mixing bowl, combine sugars, margarine or butter, sour cream, vanilla, and eggs; blend well. Add flour, baking soda, and baking powder. Gently stir in the cranberries and nuts. Do not overmix. Drop by teaspoonful 2 inches apart onto lightly greased cookie sheets. Bake for 11 to 13 minutes or until golden brown. Let cool, then frost with icing. Yields 5 dozen.

Icing:
2 c. powdered sugar
2 T. margarine, melted
1 t. grated orange peel zest
2 to 3 T. orange juice

In a small mixing bowl, blend all ingredients and spread over cooled cookies.

Snickerdoodles

This recipe is real old-fashioned and simple, and brings back so many fond memories for me of going to my grandma's house in Ohio. As soon as we walked in the back door we could smell these cookies that she always kept in a tin in the pantry. Sometimes on a blustery winter afternoon, I'll make these cookies, put on a pot of coffee or tea, and just sit for a while and remember grandma.

½ c. shortening or butter, softened
¾ c. granulated sugar
1 egg
1¼ c. flour
¼ t. salt
½ t. baking soda
1 t. cream of tartar
cinnamon and sugar

Cream shortening (or butter) and sugar. Beat in egg. Sift dry ingredients together and add to creamed mixture; stir. Refrigerate for one hour. Roll dough into walnut-sized balls and roll in the cinnamon and sugar. Place on ungreased cookie sheet and bake at 400° for 10 minutes. Cool on wire rack. Yields 2 dozen.

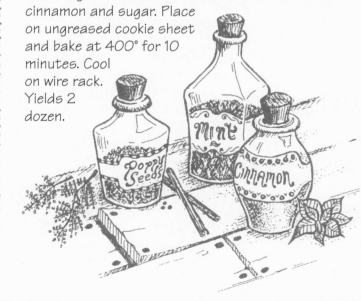

Night Before Christmas Mice

For a special gift, include a copy of *The Night Before Christmas* and flavored hot cocoa mix!

¾ c. sugar
½ c. butter or margarine, softened
½ c. shortening
1 t. vanilla
1 egg
2¼ c. all-purpose flour
¼ c. unsweetened cocoa powder
½ t. baking powder
mini semisweet baking chips
red or black string licorice cut into 2-inch pieces

Preheat oven to 325°. Beat sugar, butter, and shortening until fluffy. Add vanilla and egg; blend well. When measuring flour, lightly spoon into measuring cup and level off. Stir in flour, cocoa, and baking powder. Mix well. Shape dough into one-inch balls. To form mouse, pinch one end of ball to form nose. Make two tiny balls of dough and flatten slightly for ears. Gently press into dough on upper front of each mouse. Press two mini chocolate chips into dough below ears, for eyes. Place 2 inches apart on ungreased cookie sheet. Bake 8 to 10 minutes or until set. Immediately press licorice into the mouse for a tail. Remove and cool on wax paper. Yields 3 dozen. Adorable!

> Cookie cutters can be used to cut shapes out of cheese and lunch meat for children. They love it!

Elves' Belly Buttons

Kids of all ages get a kick out of these!

¾ c. shortening
½ c. sugar
3-oz. box lime gelatin
2 eggs
1 t. almond extract
2½ c. all-purpose flour
pinch salt
1 t. baking powder
red cinnamon candies or maraschino cherries, quartered

Cream shortening, sugar, and gelatin together. Beat eggs in and add almond extract. Mix remaining dry ingredients together and add gradually to creamed mixture, stirring well. Chill dough overnight. When ready to bake, shape dough into small balls and roll in granulated sugar. Place on greased baking sheet. Make indentation in cookie with thumb and place red cinnamon candy or quartered cherries in depression. Bake at 375° for 10 minutes. Yields 3 to 4 dozen.

Rum Balls

A very sophisticated addition to a plate of cookies.

1 c. chocolate wafer crumbs
1 c. pecans, chopped
1 c. powdered sugar
1½ T. white syrup or honey
¼ c. rum or bourbon

Mix all ingredients. Form into small balls and roll in more chopped nuts or powdered sugar. Yields about 6 dozen.

Apple Grunt

The mouth-watering aroma of apples and cinnamon will bring the whole family running!

3 T. butter
½ c. sugar
1 egg
1¼ c. all-purpose flour
½ t. baking soda
1 t. baking powder
½ t. salt
½ c. buttermilk
2¼ c. apples, peeled and diced

Brown Sugar Topping:
⅓ c. brown sugar
1 T. flour
½ t. cinnamon
2 T. butter, softened

Preheat oven to 425°. Cream together the butter and sugar. Beat in the egg. Sift together the flour, soda, baking powder, and salt. Add to the creamed mixture alternately with the buttermilk. Stir in the apples. Pour into an 8" x 8" baking dish or pan. Mix topping ingredients together until crumbly. Sprinkle over top of apple mixture. Bake for 30 minutes. Yields 6 to 8 servings.

Lace Roll-Ups

These cookies are delicate and delightful...dip them in chocolate for a special touch!

1 c. all-purpose flour
1 c. nuts, finely chopped
½ c. corn syrup
½ c. shortening
⅔ c. packed brown sugar

Preheat oven to 375°. Combine flour and nuts. In a medium saucepan over medium heat, boil corn syrup, shortening and sugar, stirring constantly. Remove from heat; gradually stir in flour-nut mixture. Drop dough by teaspoonfuls about 3 inches apart onto lightly greased baking sheet. Bake only 8 or 9 cookies at one time. Bake about 5 minutes; cool for 3 minutes before removing from baking sheet. While warm, carefully roll cookies into cylindrical shapes. If cookies harden before shaping, return them to the oven for just a moment. Yields about 4 dozen.

For chocolate dipped cookies, dip one end of the lace roll-ups in melted semisweet chocolate. Let cool.

Chocolate Torte

Answers the prayers of chocolate lovers!

1 c. pecans, toasted and chopped
24 vanilla wafers, crushed
½ c. butter
1 c. powdered sugar
1½ oz. unsweetened chocolate
1 t. vanilla
3 eggs, separated

Mix nuts and vanilla wafers, and distribute half of this mixture in bottom of 8" × 8" pan. Cream butter with sugar. Melt chocolate and stir into butter mixture. Add yolks to chocolate mixture one at a time. Add vanilla. Beat egg whites until stiff and fold into chocolate mixture. Gently spread over crumb mixture in pan. Distribute remainder of crumbs on top. Refrigerate overnight. Cut in squares and serve with whipped cream.

Lemon Chess Bars

Two layers of lemon heaven!

Bottom layer:
½ c. butter or margarine, softened
¼ c. powdered sugar
1 c. sifted all-purpose flour

Preheat oven to 350°. Cream butter with mixer. Add sugar and flour. Mix well. Place into an 8" × 8" pan and pat down. Bake for 20 minutes.

Top layer:
2 eggs
1 c. sugar
2 T. flour
3 T. lemon juice
grated rind of
**   1 lemon**

Beat all ingredients together.
Pour over baked bottom layer (not necessary to cool bottom layer). Bake 25 minutes more or until center is set. Cool. Sprinkle with powdered sugar. Cut into bars. These freeze well. Yields one dozen bars.

Chocolate Chip Cream Cheese Bars

About eight years ago I retired from the "world of business" and went back to my first profession as a nurse in the operating room of a small community hospital. What a wonderful group I worked with! Christmas rolled around and goodies baked by my coworkers appeared almost daily. Then came a day I'll never forget. Yummy chocolate chip cheese cake bars. They were heavenly! We all wanted to know who baked them, but no one would confess and take the praise. Then Hal owned up to it…a gruff, short-tempered, cigarette-smoking, coffee-drinking, pool-playing, ex-Army air corps medic. Even though Hal is no longer with us, his Chocolate Chip Cream Cheese Bars remain an all-time favorite!

1 roll refrigerated chocolate chip cookie dough
8-oz pkg. cream cheese
1 egg
½ to ¾ c. sugar

Pat out half of the dough into a 9-inch square pan. Mix cream cheese, egg, and sugar until smooth. Spread over dough. Top with remaining cookie dough. Bake until toothpick comes out clean at temperature recommended on the dough. Quick, easy, and yummy! Yields one dozen bars.

Seven-Layer Bars

This recipe is easily doubled for a 13" × 9" pan.

½ c. margarine or butter
1 c. graham cracker crumbs
6 oz. chocolate chips
6 oz. butterscotch chips or raspberry chocolate chips
1 c. flaked coconut
1 can sweetened condensed milk
1 c. walnuts or pecans, chopped

Preheat oven to 325°. Put melted margarine or butter in a glass pan (approximately 11" × 7"). Sprinkle graham cracker crumbs to coat the bottom. Evenly spread out the chocolate chips, then coconut, then butterscotch chips. Pour the condensed milk over top to coat evenly. Top with nuts. Bake for 25 to 30 minutes. Cool until almost cold and then cut with a knife or pizza cutter into small bars. Yields one dozen bars.

Fill gift baskets with easy-to-make gifts of food from the Christmas kitchen…spiced nuts, herbal vinegars, jams and jellies, homemade pickles, nut breads, and holiday cookies.

Patrick's Chocolate Brownies

Baking cookies is a favorite pastime I've enjoyed for more than 30 years. Although I make a wide variety of cookies, chocolate brownies are the best loved and most requested. During the month of December, I fill small holiday treat bags with these delicious brownies. I arrange the bags on a tray and keep it near the front door to have on hand as a holiday surprise for service and delivery people. Last year I gave a bag of brownies to our 12-year-old paper boy, Patrick, when he collected our monthly payment. Two days later he returned, and nervously inquired as to whether I had paid him because our name wasn't checked off in his record book. "Don't you remember? I gave you a bag of brownies when I paid you," I said, pointing to the tray. His freckled face reddened and he sheepishly admitted he hadn't told the truth. "I just had to have another bag of those awesome brownies!" he blurted out. His roundabout compliment warmed my heart and I handed him an extra bag as a reward for his honesty, along with the admonishment to "just ask next time." I hope you enjoy the brownies as much as Patrick!

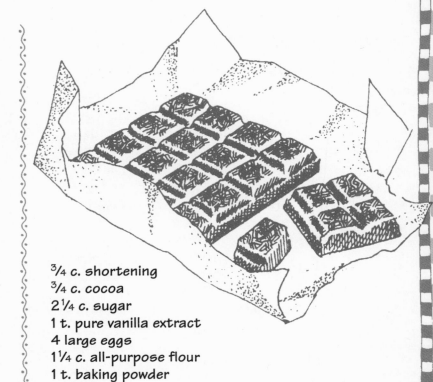

¾ c. shortening
¾ c. cocoa
2¼ c. sugar
1 t. pure vanilla extract
4 large eggs
1¼ c. all-purpose flour
1 t. baking powder
1 t. salt

Preheat the oven to 350° and grease a 13" × 9" × 2" baking pan. Melt shortening in a large saucepan over low heat, then stir in cocoa. Remove from heat. Mix in sugar and vanilla, then mix in eggs one at a time. Stir in remaining ingredients. Bake for 30 minutes. Cool completely before cutting into 2" × 2" squares. Yields 28 brownies.

When I give cookies as gifts, I like to include the recipe. I make my own recipe cards by cutting small hearts out of material with pinking shears and gluing them onto lined note cards. These recipe cards give your gift a country touch. I then tie the cards to my gift with jute string.

Brownie Trifle

This is a really easy recipe but it looks like you went to a lot of trouble. It must be made ahead, so it's a convenient, yet very elegant, end to a dinner party.

19.8-oz. pkg. fudge brownie mix
3.5-oz. pkg. instant chocolate mousse mix
eight 1.4-oz. chocolate-covered toffee bars, crushed
12-oz. container frozen whipped topping, thawed

Prepare brownie mix and bake according to package directions in a 13" × 9" pan. Let cool and crumble. Prepare chocolate mousse according to package directions, but do not chill. Place half of the crumbled brownies in the bottom of a 3-quart trifle dish. Top with half of the mousse, half of the crushed candy bars, and half of the whipped topping. Repeat layers with remaining ingredients, ending with the whipped topping. Garnish with chocolate curls if desired. Chill 8 hours. Yields 16 to 18 servings.

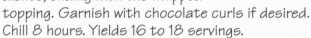

Lots of people have tree-trimming parties. Why not have a taking-down-the-tree party? Let everyone help, and make it fun. It sure beats one lone person tackling the job! Be sure to pass around the last of the holiday goodies too.

Better-than-Tollhouse Chocolate Chip Hearts

The ultimate chocolate chip cookies!

1 c. butter
½ c. granulated sugar
1 c. brown sugar, packed
2 eggs, beaten
1 T. vanilla
½ t. salt
¾ t. baking powder
2 c. all-purpose flour
½ c. quick-cooking oats
12 oz. (scant 2 c.) semisweet chocolate chips
6 oz. (scant 1 c.) milk chocolate chips or bar, broken
1 c. roasted almonds or walnuts, chopped
melted chocolate (optional)

Preheat oven to 350°. Cream butter until light. Beat in granulated sugar and brown sugar. Add beaten eggs, vanilla, salt, and baking powder; mix well. Add flour and oats and mix well. Fold in semisweet and milk chocolate chips, then the nuts. Spoon dough into greased and floured small heart-shaped (disposable foil pans work well) cake pans (about ⅓ to ½ cup dough for 4" × 5" heart pans). Bake for 12 to 15 minutes or until lightly browned. Bake longer if filling pans more fully for cakelike cookies. Or, drop dough by large spoonfuls onto greased baking sheet and bake at 350° for 10 minutes. Let stand for 5 minutes in pans then cut along side with knife and turn over pan, tapping lightly on center of pan until released. Let cool. If desired, frost with melted chocolate. Yields 20 to 24 large heart cookies or 4 dozen round cookies.

Old-Fashioned Fruitcake

Make this a few weeks before Christmas for a truly savory fruitcake.

2 c. pecan halves
¾ lb. candied pineapple
¾ lb. candied cherries, whole
1½ lbs. ready mix candied fruit
1 lb. seedless raisins
½ lb. butter
2½ c. sugar
6 eggs
1-oz. bottle brandy flavoring
4 c. flour
1 t. salt
1½ t. cinnamon
1 t. nutmeg

Line an angel food cake pan with foil. Have nuts and fruit ready. Mix butter, sugar, eggs, and flavoring in a large bowl with electric mixer. Sift together flour, salt, cinnamon, and nutmeg, and mix thoroughly with butter and egg mixture. Work the fruits and nuts into batter with hands. Be sure to leave some pecans behind for decoration. Fill pan two-thirds full with batter. Bake at 275° for 3 hours. One-half hour before cake is done, brush top with light corn syrup. Decorate with pecan halves and finish baking. Cool. Wrap in a brandy-soaked cloth, and place in an airtight container. Store in a cool place for several weeks to blend and mellow the cake.

Grandma Liz's Pumpkin Pie

This was my mother-in-law's recipe. It is not an orange pie, but very dark and rich because of all the spices. I don't eat "orange" pumpkin pies anymore!

1¼ c. milk
½ c. brown sugar, packed
1 T. cooking oil
¼ t. each: ginger, nutmeg, and cloves
½ t. each: cinnamon, allspice and salt
1¼ c. cooked and strained pumpkin
    (canned is fine)
2 eggs
prebaked 9-inch pie shell

Scald milk and when it has cooled to warm, stir in the brown sugar. In a bowl, mix oil, spices and salt with the pumpkin; add the eggs; then add the milk-brown sugar mixture, mixing thoroughly. Pour mixture into pie crust and bake 50 to 60 minutes in a 350° oven. Check center of pie to make sure it is done. When making 2 pies, use 5 eggs.

Not-So-Sweet Pecan Pie

My mom has had this recipe since the early 1930s. She still makes it and she is 85!

¾ c. sugar
¾ c. white corn syrup
2 t. vanilla
⅛ t. salt
1 T. flour
3 T. margarine, melted
2 c. pecans, slightly broken
3 eggs, beaten
unbaked 9-inch pie crust (see below)

Preheat oven to 300°. Mix all ingredients except the eggs. Beat the eggs with an electric mixer and add to mixture. Pour into 9-inch pie crust and bake at 300° for 40 minutes, then turn oven up to 350° and bake for an additional 15 to 20 minutes. I sometimes put in ½ cup of chocolate chips for a different, yummy flavor.

Crust:
1 c. flour
½ t. salt
⅓ c. vegetable
    shortening
3 T. cold water

Using pastry cutter, blend flour, salt, and shortening. Stir in water and roll out crust.

The Best Apple Walnut Raisin Pie

The title says it all!

10-inch pie crust
3 tart red apples, peeled and thinly sliced
1¼ c. water
¾ c. plus 2 T. sugar
2 T. cornstarch
¾ c. graham cracker crumbs
½ c. butter, room temperature
6 to 8 T. dark raisins
¼ c. walnuts, chopped
1 T. fresh lemon juice
¼ t. vanilla
pinch each of: cinnamon, mace, and nutmeg

Arrange apples over crust. Place rack in middle of oven and preheat to 400°. Combine one cup of water and ¾ cup sugar in small saucepan; bring to a boil over medium heat, stirring until sugar dissolves; then boil 10 minutes more without stirring. Add cornstarch dissolved in remaining water, and stir constantly until thickened. Pour over apples. Thoroughly combine crumbs, butter, raisins, and walnuts. Mix in remaining ingredients and sprinkle evenly over apples. Bake 15 minutes. Cover with foil, and bake 30 minutes longer. Serve warm.

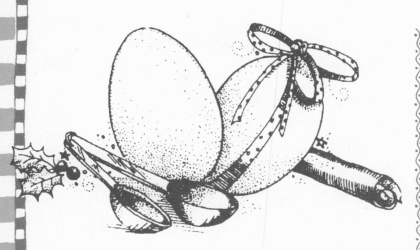

Christmas Cheesecake

This recipe has the advantage of making delicious cheesecake without the bother of a springform pan.

Crust:
½ c. all-purpose flour
⅓ c. butter, softened
½ c. brown sugar

Combine all ingredients. Pat in an ungreased 8-inch-square pan (or use a round pan). Bake at 350° for 8 to 10 minutes. Remove from oven.

Filling:
two 8-oz pkgs. cream cheese, softened
½ c. sugar
2 large eggs
4 T. milk or cream
2 T. lemon juice
1 t. vanilla

Using an electric mixer, combine all ingredients until smooth. Spread over partially baked crust. Bake 30 to 35 minutes more at 350°.

Out-of-This-World Fudge Topping

A real treat for the chocolate lover, but don't count the calories.

vegetable oil spray
½ c. butter
¾ c. cocoa powder
2 c. sugar
⅛ t. salt
¾ c. evaporated milk
7 oz. marshmallow cream
1 t. vanilla extract
1 c. walnuts, chopped

In a 4-quart saucepan sprayed with vegetable oil spray, melt butter over low heat. Stir in the cocoa and add sugar, salt, and evaporated milk. Stir until well-blended. Add marshmallow cream and bring to a boil. Boil for about 5 minutes, stirring constantly. Remove from the heat and stir in the vanilla. Cool about 20 minutes and beat with a wooden spoon. Stir in the walnuts. Spoon into small jars and refrigerate. When ready to serve, set jar in a little hot water until it is pourable. Serve over ice cream or angel food cake.

Use your cookie cutters for cutting out tea sandwiches. Mix cream cheese with fresh herbs, spread between two pieces of cocktail bread and cut out hearts, bells, stars...whatever suits the occasion!

Get Your Moose Chocolate Style

A real chocolate mousse pie, that is!

This is an original recipe developed and written by my dad. He gave it to me years ago and I have handed it down to my daughter. He definitely has his own style.

3-oz. pkg. cream cheese
1 ready-made pie crust (any type, but I like
    graham cracker best!)
8-oz. container frozen whipped topping
½ c. sugar
1 t. vanilla
⅓ c. cocoa
⅓ c. milk

Before gettin' started on this masterpiece, get the cream cheese out of the fridge and the frozen whipped topping out of the freezer. Let these come to room temperature for an hour or two. While they're warmin' up, you can put all the other stuff out on your work bench...won't hurt anything! Remove the plastic cover from your pie crust and wash it, so when you cover your finished product with it, the clean side will be toward the mousse pie. Keep the pie crust in its aluminum container nearby, ready to receive the filling. Get a mixing bowl, oh, about the size that will hold 2 quarts of water. I use a wooden spoon to do the mixing that follows, but you could use an electric mixer (remember, it's easier to lick the spoon than those gadgets on the electric mixer!). Dump in the cream cheese, sugar, vanilla, cocoa, and then the milk and start mixin' it. Better do it so that the milk is last 'cause it'll all mix easier. Do it near your sink in case you splatter, like I do. I admit that it takes longer to use the wooden spoon, but I'm not in a hurry! After it looks pretty well mixed, start adding the whipped topping a few spoonfuls at a time and keep mixin'. Finally get all the whipped topping mixed in. When you think you've done your best mixing job, carefully dump it into the ready-made pie crust. Now put the clean plastic cover on this beauty, and put it in your freezer or fridge. Personally, I like it best when it's frozen like ice cream. OK, now the fun starts... thoroughly lick the spoon and mixin' bowl! Oh yes, be sure to share the pie.

Mom's Carrot Cake

The crushed pineapple gives this cake a moist-ness you can't resist!

2 c. sugar
2 c. all-purpose flour
2 t. baking soda
1 t. salt
3 t. cinnamon
16-oz. can crushed pineapple, drained
1½ c. vegetable oil
4 eggs
3 c. carrots, grated
½ c. pecans, chopped

Preheat oven to 350°. Grease and flour a 11" × 9" cake pan. Mix sugar, flour, baking soda, salt, and cinnamon in small bowl. Set aside. Mix pineapple, oil, eggs, and carrots. Beat in dry ingredients. Fold in pecans. Pour into pan and bake 30 to 35 minutes, or until center is done. Apply frosting when cool.

Frosting:
½ c. butter
8 oz. cream cheese
1 box powdered sugar
2 t. vanilla extract
½ c. pecans

Beat butter and cream cheese until smooth. Blend in powdered sugar and vanilla. Fold in pecans.

Heavenly Black Forest Cake

Quick and easy, but it tastes like it took all day to make.

1 pkg. devil's food cake mix
3 large eggs
1 can cherry pie filling
1 t. vanilla extract
1 T. real sour cream or vegetable oil
¾ c. milk

Preheat oven to 350°. Combine everything in a mixing bowl and beat together. If batter seems too thick, add a splash of water. Pour into a greased bundt or tube pan, or into two-layer pans. Bake 45 to 55 minutes for bundt or tube pans; 25 minutes for layer pans. It is done when the top springs back when touched. Turn onto a pretty dish and sprinkle with powdered sugar, or ice as follows: Mix a box of vanilla instant pudding as directions indicate. Fold in a small container of whipped topping (the more topping, the lighter the frosting). Spread over the cake.

Decorating idea: Take large marshmallows and cut in half with scissors. Put the cut side into some red sugar. Place a piece of citrus peel in the middle and make a flower. Add green spearmint leaves and decorate the top of the cake however you like. Looks very festive! Refrigerate until serving.

Merry Berry Almond Glazed Sour Cream Cake

Red berries peeking through the almonds make this a particularly festive-looking cake.

2 c. all-purpose flour
1 t. baking powder
1 t. baking soda
½ t. salt
½ c. butter or margarine, softened
1 c. sugar
2 large eggs
2 t. almond extract
1½ c. sour cream
16-oz. can whole cranberry sauce
½ c. almonds chopped

Glaze:
¾ c. powdered sugar
2 T. warm water
½ t. almond extract

Preheat oven to 350°. Grease and flour a 10-inch tube pan. Mix flour, baking powder, soda, and salt together and set aside. Cream butter and sugar together, beating well. Add eggs, beating very well after each egg is added. Mix in almond extract. Stir in flour mixture, alternating with the sour cream. Spoon half of the batter into the prepared tube pan. Spoon half of the cranberry sauce over the batter and swirl slightly. Spoon remaining batter over swirled cranberry sauce. Cover this batter with remaining cranberry sauce, swirling slightly. Sprinkle with almonds. Bake at 350° for 45 to 55 minutes, until firm. Cool 10 minutes and carefully remove from pan and glaze.

For glaze: Mix powdered sugar, warm water, and almond extract together and carefully pour over the top of the cake.

Fa-la-la-la la-la-la-la-la
At your neighborhood Christmas party, invite the local high school choir to come caroling. This will be a delightful surprise for all the guests!

'Twas the Night Before Christmas Dinner

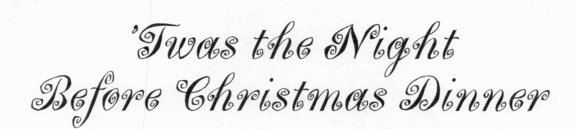

Baked Artichokes with Mustard Butter Sauce

Prime Rib Roast with Yorkshire Pudding

Creamed Onions with Peanuts

Sour Cream Mashed Potatoes

Glazed Carrots

Lentil & Mushroom Loaf

Pears with Cranberry Relish

Broccoli Casserole

Frozen Christmas Salad

Candied Oranges

Mint-Filled Chocolate Cups

Walnut Torte

Christmas Wassail

Smiling Bishops

Baked Artichokes with Mustard Butter Sauce

Give yourselves plenty of time to savor this delectable appetizer!

6 artichokes (1 per person), cleaned and trimmed
1 clove garlic, minced
3 T. olive oil
salt and pepper to taste
seasoned bread crumbs

Sauce:
2 shallots, minced
1 c. dry white wine
1 c. heavy cream
½ lb. unsalted butter, softened
2 T. Dijon mustard
salt and pepper to taste

Cut off the stems of the artichokes flush with the bottoms so they'll stand upright. Trim the points off the leaves with scissors. Place in a large pan and cover with cold water. Season the water with the garlic and one tablespoon of olive oil. (Place a heavy plate on top of the artichokes so they won't float to the top.)

Simmer for 40 minutes, or until the leaves pull away easily. Drain and cool. Place in a covered casserole with ½ inch water in the bottom and sprinkle bread crumbs inside the artichokes, separating the leaves out gently as you go. Drizzle with remaining olive oil. Bake the artichokes, covered, in a 375° F oven for about 15 minutes. Meanwhile, prepare the sauce by placing the shallots with the wine in a sauté pan. Simmer until wine is reduced by half. Add the cream and simmer until very thick. Whisk in the butter and mustard and season with salt and pepper. When the artichokes are heated through, pour some sauce on individual plates and put an artichoke on each plate. To eat, pull the leaves free with your fingers, dip into the sauce, and scrape the soft white part of the leaf off with your teeth. When you get near the heart of the artichoke, the leaves will be so tender you can eat them whole. Once you have reached the heart, scrape off the white "beard" and eat the tender heart with a fork. Delicious!

fresh HERBS

Prime Rib Roast

A glorious roast of prime rib, crusty on the outside, juicy and pink in the middle, makes the perfect holiday feast. Yorkshire pudding, steeped in tradition, is an easy recipe that adds that special touch.

5 lb. prime beef rib roast
freshly ground pepper to taste

Trim roast of fat and place on its rib bones in an open roasting pan. Sprinkle with pepper to taste. Roast in 325° oven until temperature on a meat thermometer registers 140° (for rare); about 2 hours.

Yorkshire Pudding

2 large eggs
1 c. milk
½ t. salt
1 c. all-purpose flour, sifted
13 ¾-oz. can beef broth
parsley sprigs

Remove the roast from the oven. In a mixing bowl, whisk eggs until foamy. Beat in milk and salt. Gradually beat in flour until mixture is smooth. The last 30 minutes of baking, raise the oven temperature to 400°, add broth, and pour the batter around the roast. (Keep an eye on the meat thermometer to make sure you don't overcook the roast!) Cut pudding into squares and arrange around roast when serving. Garnish with parsley. Yields 8 to 10 servings.

Creamed Onions with Peanuts

This southern dish is full of flavor and crunchy texture.

20 whole small white onions, peeled
2 T. butter
2 T. all-purpose flour
2 c. milk
¼ c. whole and ¼ c. coarsely chopped salted peanuts
½ c. bread crumbs

Cook onions in boiling salted water until tender. Drain. Melt butter in a small saucepan and stir in flour. Add milk and cook over medium heat, stirring until smooth and thickened. Put onions in a greased casserole dish and pour the sauce over them. Stir in the whole peanuts. Top with bread crumbs and chopped peanuts. Bake at 400° for 15 minutes, or until lightly browned. Yields 6 to 8 servings.

"Oh! What a wonderful pudding!" Bob Cratchit said, and calmly too, that he regarded it as the greatest success achieved by Mrs. Cratchit since their marriage.
—Charles Dickens, *A Christmas Carol*

Sour Cream Mashed Potatoes

These baked mashed potatoes are an old favorite.

5 lbs. russet or Yukon Gold potatoes, peeled
  and cut into cubes
2 T. butter
1 c. sour cream
4 strips of bacon, cooked crisp and crumbled
salt and pepper to taste

Cover the potatoes with cold salted water and bring to a boil, simmering 20 minutes or until tender. Drain and mash with a potato masher or ricer. Whisk in the butter and sour cream and season to taste. Sprinkle with crumbled bacon. Transfer to a greased baking dish and bake for 10 to 15 minutes. Yields 10 servings.

Glazed Carrots

Carrots add a cheerful, bright splash of color and flavor to any meal.

2 T. onion, chopped
2 T. parsley, chopped
2 T. butter
8 carrots, peeled and quartered
10½ oz. can beef consommé
¼ t. sugar

Sauté onion and parsley in butter until tender. Add carrots, consommé, and sugar. Cover and cook 5 minutes. Uncover and cook 10 minutes more, or until carrots are crisp yet tender. Sprinkle with a little nutmeg if you like. Yields 8 servings.

Rinse and sort the lentils. Combine in a heavy saucepan with 4 cups of water. Bring to a boil, then lower the heat and simmer, covered, until the lentils are tender, about 45 minutes. Drain. Preheat the oven to 350°. Heat the oil in a large skillet. Add the garlic and mushrooms and sauté over medium heat, stirring, until the mushrooms are wilted. Stir in the spinach, lentils, soy sauce, and wheat germ. Grind in some pepper, to taste, and add the nutmeg. Cook, stirring, until the mixture is heated through, then stir in the cheese. Lightly oil a 9" × 5" × 3" loaf pan, preferably glass. Pour in about two-thirds of the lentil mixture. Press some of the mixture up the sides of the pan to create a shell about ½-inch thick. Transfer the remaining lentil mixture to a small bowl and reserve until needed.

Lentil & Mushroom Loaf with Savory Potato Filling

The vegetarians at your holiday gathering will thank you for this one…and don't be surprised if everyone else enjoys it, too!

1 c. raw lentils
1 T. safflower oil
2 cloves garlic, minced
6 oz. white mushrooms, sliced
5 oz. frozen spinach, thawed
1 T. natural soy sauce
2 T. wheat germ
freshly ground pepper
dash nutmeg
1 c. firmly packed Stilton or Gruyère cheese,
    grated

Filling:
1 T. safflower oil
1 c. onion, chopped
¼ c. dry bread crumbs
½ t. dried thyme
freshly ground pepper, to taste
1 c. coarsely mashed potato (from about
    1 medium cooked and peeled potato)
½ t. seasoned salt
½ t. dried basil
curly parsley for garnish

Rinse the skillet and heat the oil. Add the onion and sauté until golden brown. Add the remaining filling ingredients and sauté, stirring occasionally, for 5 minutes. Transfer into the prepared shell, then cover the top with the reserved lentil mixture. Bake for 40 to 45 minutes, or until the top is crusty. Remove from the oven and let the loaf stand for 10 to 15 minutes. Slide a spatula or knife around the edges to loosen it. Cut slices and arrange them on an oblong dish. Garnish with parsley and serve.

Pears with Cranberry Relish

A light, refreshing, healthful medley of fruit colors and flavors.

12-oz. pkg. fresh cranberries
2 unpeeled red apples, cored
  and quartered
1 unpeeled lemon, quartered
  and seeded
1½ c. sugar
6 fresh, ripe Bartlett pears

In a food processor, process cranberries, apples, and lemon using medium blade until well chopped. Stir in sugar. Cover and chill in refrigerator. Cut pears in half lengthwise and hollow out each half with the tip of a spoon. Spoon the relish into the pears and serve. Yields 12 servings.

Broccoli Casserole

Try half broccoli and half cauliflower for a different version of this casserole. Delicious!

1 regular and 1 large bag of frozen broccoli
2 boxes chicken flavored rice vermicelli mix
2 cans cream of chicken soup
16 oz. pasteurized processed cheese spread

Cook broccoli according to package directions, and then prepare rice vermicelli mix according to package directions. Place cooked broccoli in a 4-quart slow cooker. Add cream of chicken soup to broccoli and stir. Cut up cheese, and add to mixture in slow cooker and stir. Stir in rice vermicelli mix. Allow time in heated slow cooker for cheese to melt, and serve. Yields approximately thirty-two 4-oz. servings.

Frozen Christmas Salad

So cool and creamy!

¾ of 16-oz. bag miniature marshmallows
20-oz. can crushed pineapple, drained
½ c. mayonnaise or salad dressing
8-oz. pkg. cream cheese
12 ea. red and green maraschino cherries, chopped
½ c. English walnuts, chopped
1 c. whipping cream, whipped

Combine marshmallows and pineapple; set aside until marshmallows are well soaked. Mix salad dressing and cream cheese and combine with pineapple mixture. Add chopped cherries and nuts. Whip the whipping cream and fold into the salad. Pour into mold or container of your choice and freeze. Cut and serve on a lettuce leaf. Yields 10 servings.

Carve out apples, oranges, and artichokes and tuck in votive candles. Candles everywhere say "welcome."

Candied Oranges

A canister of candied oranges makes a lovely hostess gift.

1⅓ c. sugar
4 c. water
1 T. vanilla
1 t. ground cinnamon
½ t. ground nutmeg
6 seedless oranges, with skin lightly scored to release oils
juice of 1 lemon
1 c. whipped cream
2 T. brandy

Combine sugar, water, vanilla, cinnamon, and nutmeg in a large, heavy pot. Bring to a boil, reduce heat to low, cover, and simmer for 20 minutes. Add the oranges, making sure they are covered about three-quarters of the way up by the syrup. Cover and slowly cook oranges for 2 hours, turning a few times during cooking. Remove pot from heat and add lemon juice. Place cover back on pot and allow mixture to chill overnight. To serve, slice oranges into wheels and arrange on a pretty plate. Top with whipped cream flavored with brandy.

Mint-Filled Chocolate Cups

Mint and chocolate are the perfect after-dinner companions.

1 c. vegetable shortening
¾ c. firmly packed brown sugar
¾ c. granulated sugar
2 eggs, slightly beaten
½ c. milk
3 c. flour
1 t. baking soda
½ c. cocoa powder
½ t. salt
1 t. vanilla

Preheat oven to 375°. Grease mini-muffin pan. Cream together shortening and sugars. Add eggs, milk, and vanilla; beat well. Add sifted dry ingredients and stir well. Chill dough 15 minutes. With greased hands, roll dough into one-inch balls. Place a ball in each muffin cup and bake for 10 to 12 minutes. When done, immediately make deep indentation in each cookie with melon baller, forming a cup. Cool for 10 minutes and remove cookies from pan. Cool completely. Yields 4 to 5 dozen.

Filling:
2 cans white frosting
mint extract
red and green food coloring
sugar sprinkles, optional

Save Christmas cards for opening
at suppertime so everyone can see.

Take two small bowls and scrape one can of frosting into each bowl. Add one teaspoon of mint extract to each bowl and stir well. Add red food coloring to one bowl, and green food coloring to the other, stirring well. Frosting may be spooned into cookies or may be piped into each cookie using a pastry bag and star tip. Cookies can be topped with sugar sprinkles for an extra festive look. Cookies keep their beautiful shape best if refrigerated.

Walnut Torte

A heavenly combination of walnuts with rich coffee and a creamy filling.

3 large eggs, separated
¾ c. plus 2 T. sugar
1½ c. walnut pieces
2 T. soft, fresh bread crumbs
1 T. strongly brewed coffee
2 T. dark rum

Filling:
1½ c. heavy cream, well chilled
1½ T. instant coffee powder
¾ c. powdered sugar

Line three 9-inch round cake pans with wax paper. Then butter and flour the paper. Beat the egg yolks with ¾ c. of sugar until doubled in volume (about 5 minutes at medium-high with an electric mixer). Set mixture aside. Grind the walnuts with 2 tablespoons sugar in a food processor until very fine. Add walnuts, bread crumbs, coffee, and rum to the egg mixture and fold gently. Beat the egg whites just until stiff and fold into the egg yolk mixture. Pour the batter into the cake pans. Bake about 24 minutes, or until lightly golden. The cake should spring back when touched with a fingertip. Allow to cool about 10 minutes; loosen with a knife and place on a rack, removing the paper. When cake is completely cooled, prepare the filling.

Stir the coffee into a small amount of the cream until dissolved. Add the remaining cream and the sugar. Beat until cream is very fluffy and forms soft peaks. Spread the whipped cream over each layer and arrange toasted walnuts, or garnish of your choice, on top. Chill one hour before serving. Yields 12 servings.

Christmas Wassail

The traditional grog for singing carols 'round the piano.

1 gallon apple cider
1 qt. orange juice
1 c. fresh lemon juice
1 qt. pineapple juice
24 cloves
4 sticks cinnamon
1 c. brown sugar

Mix all the ingredients in a large pot and heat to almost boiling. Reduce heat and simmer about 45 minutes. Remove cinnamon and cloves before serving. Yields 1½ gallons.

Smiling Bishops

In the days of Victorian England, this merry mixture would put even Ebeneezer Scrooge into the holiday spirit!

1 bottle port
1 bottle red wine
1 orange, sliced
8 whole cloves

Heat all ingredients until simmering and strain into mugs. Yields 10 to 12 servings.

Our family has been keeping a "Holiday Memory" photo book of all the Christmas parties and dinners for over 25 years. The children and grandchildren love to page through all the memories of good times shared...a wonderful legacy to pass on.

Christmas Is Here
Breakfast or Brunch

Vanilla Coffee

Sunrise Punch

Applesauce Muffins

Christmas Casserole

Skiers' French Toast

Honey Spiced Ham

Cranberry-Orange Chutney

Christmas Morning Sticky Buns

Pumpkin Nut Bread

Vanilla Coffee

Provides a rich, mellow wake-up on Christmas Day.

1½ c. milk
1 T. sugar
½ t. ground cinnamon
3 c. hot, strong brewed
    coffee
1½ t. pure vanilla extract
whipped topping

Combine milk, sugar, and cinnamon in a saucepan and stir well. Cook over medium heat 2 minutes, or until sugar dissolves. Remove from heat; stir in coffee and vanilla. Pour into mugs and garnish with whipped topping. Sprinkle with cinnamon. Yields 4 servings.

Sunrise Punch

A festive brunch drink for a special occasion.

3 c. unsweetened orange juice
½ c. plus 2 T. tequila
¼ c. fresh lime juice
2 T. powdered sugar
2 T. orange-flavored liqueur
1 T. grenadine syrup (optional)
lime slices

Combine orange juice, tequila, lime juice, sugar, and liqueur in a pitcher, and chill. Fill 6 tall glasses with ice and pour in mixture. Slowly add ½ teaspoon grenadine down the inside of each glass, if desired. Garnish with lime slices.

Applesauce Muffins

Great for breakfast, brunch, snacks, or with dinner.

1 c. margarine
1 c. white sugar
1 c. brown sugar
2 large eggs
1 c. chopped nuts
3 t. cinnamon
2 t. baking soda
1 t. allspice
½ t. salt
4 c. all-purpose flour
2 c. applesauce

Preheat oven to 400°. Cream margarine. Blend in sugars and eggs. Add nuts, cinnamon, soda, allspice and salt. Mix well. Add flour and applesauce. Bake for 15 to 18 minutes. Yields about 3 dozen.

Note: Batter can be microwaved on high for 2 to 3 minutes (remember to rotate pan). Also, batter can be kept in the refrigerator for 2 weeks. Just stir it up and bake.

Surround your holiday punch bowl with greenery, berries, shiny red apples, golden pears, and spicy pomanders!

Christmas Casserole

A Christmas Day favorite. Make it the day before and just pop it in the oven!

5½ oz. seasoned croutons
1 lb. bulk sausage, cooked, crumbled, and drained
4 eggs
2 c. milk
1 can cream of mushroom soup
16 oz. frozen Italian vegetables
1 c. Cheddar cheese, shredded
1 c. Monterey Jack cheese, shredded

Line the bottom of a 13" × 9" baking pan with the croutons. Sprinkle cooked sausage over the croutons. Beat eggs and milk until thoroughly mixed and add remaining ingredients, stirring well. Pour egg mixture over the sausage. Bake at 350° for one hour. Casserole may be prepared ahead and refrigerated before baking. Yields 8 servings.

Skiers' French Toast

For Christmas brunch serve with chilled juice, fresh fruit, Canadian bacon or sausage, and lots of wonderful strongly brewed coffee!

½ c. butter
1 c. brown sugar
2 T. dark corn syrup
1 loaf of French bread, cut into thick slices
5 eggs
1½ c. milk
2 t. vanilla
pinch of nutmeg

Cook butter, brown sugar, and corn syrup until sugar is dissolved; pour into a 13" × 9" pan. Layer bread pieces on top of syrup mixture. In a bowl, mix eggs, milk, vanilla, and nutmeg. Pour over bread. Cover and refrigerate overnight. Bake, uncovered, at 350° for 45 minutes. Serves 6 to 8.

You can use your cookie cutters for making French toast! Cut out a variety of designs from raisin bread. Dip it in batter and cook. Sift powdered sugar over top and cover with syrup. Serve with crisp bacon, fresh fruit, and juice. Also fun to cut out pancakes and folksy sandwiches too!

Honey Spiced Ham

Yummy ham for sandwiches and snacking all day long.

**10-lb. bone-in ham
cloves
½ c. honey
¼ c. butter
1 t. ground cinnamon
½ t. ground nutmeg
¼ t. allspice**

Place ham, fat side up, on a rack in a shallow roasting pan. Score in a diamond pattern about ¼-inch deep. Insert cloves in center of each diamond. Bake, uncovered, about 2 hours. Combine all remaining ingredients and cook over medium heat, stirring until mixture comes to a boil. Spread glaze over ham and bake another 15 or 20 minutes.

Cranberry–Orange Chutney

An excellent relish for ham sandwiches.

**4 seedless oranges
½ c. orange juice
1 lb. fresh cranberries
2 c. sugar
¼ c. crystallized ginger, diced
½ t. hot pepper sauce
1 cinnamon stick
1 clove garlic, peeled
3/4 t. curry powder
3/4 c. golden raisins**

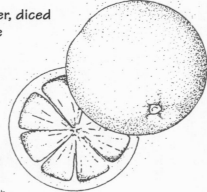

Peel the oranges and reserve the rind from two of them. Slice the reserved rind very thinly. Cut oranges in ¼-inch-thick slices and quarter. Combine orange rind with all remaining ingredients and simmer in a saucepan over moderate heat, stirring until sugar dissolves and cranberries open. Remove from heat and discard cinnamon and garlic clove. Add oranges and toss lightly. Serve hot or cold with ham. Yields 6 cups.

Christmas Morning Sticky Buns

A Christmas morning crowd pleaser!

1 pkg. frozen roll dough (18 to 20)
1 small pkg. butterscotch pudding (not instant)
½ c. sugar
2 T. cinnamon
1 c. nuts, walnuts, or pecans (optional)
1 T. butter, melted

Before going to bed on Christmas Eve, place frozen roll dough in greased bundt pan. Combine pudding mix, sugar, cinnamon, and nuts (if used). Sprinkle over frozen dough. Pour melted butter over top as evenly as possible. Cover with a towel and leave on counter overnight. In the morning, bake at 350° for 30 minutes, or until lightly brown on top. To serve, invert bundt pan on serving dish. Lift carefully as "sticky sauce" will run out. Yields 18 to 20 sticky buns.

Pumpkin Nut Bread

Easy snacking for the Christmas crowd.

3¼ c. all-purpose flour
¾ c. quick oats
2 t. baking soda
1½ t. pumpkin pie spice
½ t. baking powder
½ t. salt
3 large eggs
15-oz. can pumpkin
1½ c. granulated sugar
1½ c. packed brown sugar
½ c. water
½ c. vegetable oil
½ c. evaporated milk
1 c. walnuts, chopped

Preheat oven to 350°. Combine flour, oats, baking soda, pumpkin pie spice, baking powder, and salt in a large bowl. Beat together eggs, pumpkin, sugars, water, oil, and evaporated milk on medium speed until combined. Beat flour mixture into pumpkin mixture until blended; stir in nuts. Fill two greased 9" × 5" loaf pans and bake for 65 to 70 minutes, or until toothpick comes out clean. Cool in pans 10 minutes; remove from pans to cool completely.

We wish you a Merry Christmas
and a happy New Year;
a pocket full of money and a house full of cheer;
and a great fat pig to last you all the year.
—Traditional song

God Bless Us Every One
Christmas Banquet

Mulled Cranberry Cider

Crab Quiche Appetizers

Mushroom Logs

Baked Ham with Cherry Glaze

The Juiciest-Ever Roast Turkey

Mother's Celery Cornbread Dressing

Sweet Potato Casserole

Baby Baked Beans

Onion & Apple Casserole

Green Beans with Mushroom Sauce

Grandma Essie Hill's Blackberry Cobbler

Scottish Shortbread

Mulled Cranberry Cider

Tangy cranberry, warm and inviting.

1 small orange
8 c. cranberry-raspberry drink
¼ c. light brown sugar
orange peel cut into strips
6-inch cinnamon stick
1 t. whole cloves
1 star anise
8-inch square of cheesecloth

Using a vegetable peeler, remove orange peel and set aside. Squeeze the juice from the orange, discard seeds and pulp. In a large saucepan combine cranberry-raspberry drink and brown sugar. In an 8-inch square of cheesecloth, combine most of the orange peel strips, cinnamon, whole cloves, and star anise. Tie cheesecloth with cotton twine. Add to liquid. Bring mixture to a boil; reduce heat. Cover and simmer for 10 minutes. Remove from heat and discard spices. Serve warm, garnished with additional orange peel.

Crab Quiche Appetizers

Set these out and watch them disappear!

2 refrigerated pie crusts
8 oz. crab flakes or chunks
4 eggs, beaten
1½ c. half-and-half
¼ t. dill weed
1½ c. Swiss cheese, shredded
½ c. Parmesan cheese

Preheat oven to 450°. Unfold and gently roll out both pie crusts. Arrange crusts slightly overlapping to cover bottom and sides of a greased 15" × 10" jelly roll pan. Crimp edges; prick bottom and sides. Bake 10 to 12 minutes or until golden brown. Reduce oven temperature to 350°. Cover bottom of crust with crab. Mix eggs, half-and-half, and dill until blended. Add cheeses and pour over seafood. Bake 30 minutes. Cut into squares. Yields approximately 5 dozen.

Mushroom Logs

Delicious tidbits—save room for dinner!

two 8-oz. cans crescent dinner rolls
8-oz. pkg. cream cheese, softened
two 4-oz. cans mushroom pieces, drained and
chopped (or 16 oz. fresh)
1 t. seasoned salt
1 bunch scallions, chopped
1 T. Worcestershire sauce
1 t. lemon pepper
1 egg, beaten
2 T. poppy seeds (optional)

Preheat oven to 375°. Separate dough into
four rectangles, pressing seams together.
Combine cream cheese with mushrooms, salt,
scallions, Worcestershire sauce, and lemon
pepper. Spread evenly over rectangles. Roll into
logs, starting with long side of rectangle. Pinch
seams. Brush with egg, and sprinkle with poppy
seeds. Cut into one-inch pieces. Place on
ungreased cookie sheet, seam side down. Bake
at 375° for 10 to 12 minutes.

Baked Ham with Cherry Glaze

A tasty alternative to turkey.

5 lb. canned ham (or any ham)
16-oz. can pitted dark sweet cherries
¼ c. sweet wine
1 T. sugar
1 T. cornstarch
1 T. lemon juice

Bake ham in 325° oven for 1½ to 2 hours. After
ham has roasted for one hour, make the glaze. Drain
cherry liquid into a one-quart saucepan, stir in sweet
wine, sugar, cornstarch, and lemon juice. Cook over
medium heat, stirring until mixture boils and thickens slightly; boil for one minute. During the last 30
minutes of baking, brush ham frequently with some
of the cherry sauce. When ham is done, arrange
slices on a warm platter. Stir cherries into remaining
sauce in saucepan. Heat thoroughly. Spoon some
cherry sauce over ham on platter. Serve remaining
sauce in a small bowl.

The Juiciest-Ever Roast Turkey

Your guests are sure to "gobble" up this winning turkey!

Marinade:
¼ c. (4 T.) dry mustard
2 T. Worcestershire sauce
¼ to ½ t. cider vinegar
2½ T. olive oil
1 t. salt
⅛ t. freshly ground pepper

Be sure to make more marinade for a bigger turkey. Combine all ingredients into a soft paste, similar to a thick marinade, and paint it all over a well-thawed turkey, inside and out, a few hours or the day before cooking.

9½ lb. turkey
1 onion
2 stalks celery, cut to fit
some parsley
2 strips of bacon
½ c. butter
olive oil
turkey or chicken broth

Instead of stuffing, place onion, celery, and parsley inside turkey. Across the breast place bacon, and in the crevice between the drumstick and the body, tuck in chunks of butter. Place the turkey in an uncovered roaster. Soak a dish towel or piece of cheesecloth in olive oil and lay it over the turkey. For basting, add one to 2 cups turkey stock from cooking the gizzard, neck, and other parts (or chicken broth). Baste at least twice through the cheesecloth during roasting. Cook at 300° (not the traditional 325°), according to this table:

7-10 lbs.	30 min. per lb.
10-15 lbs.	20 min. per lb.
15-18 lbs.	18 min. per lb.
18-20 lbs.	15 min. per lb.
20-23 lbs.	13 min. per lb.

I cook my turkey one hour more than the table recommends, but the turkey remains moist and juice. For gravy, the pan juices are abundant and richly flavorful, to thicken as you like.

Safey tips for your holiday turkey:
• Thaw in the microwave or refrigerator.
• Don't cook overnight at low temperatures. Cook at 325°.
• After it's cooked, don't leave turkey sitting out for more than 2 hours.

Mother's Celery Cornbread Dressing

Be sure to toss ingredients lightly for a nice, fluffy dressing.

14-oz. pkg. cornbread dressing mix
14-oz. pkg. herb dressing mix
8-inch square pan of baked cornbread, broken into pieces
2 eggs, beaten
1 small jar mushroom slices, drained
2 c. celery, diced
packet of chicken broth mix
poultry seasoning to taste
½ can water chestnuts, drained and sliced
⅓ c. butter
turkey broth

Mix all ingredients together lightly, using enough turkey broth to flavor dressing without making it soggy. Cook loose in uncovered pan at 350° for one hour.

Sweet Potato Casserole

An old-fashioned favorite...top with brown sugar and crushed walnuts for a festive touch.

2 lbs. sweet potatoes (5 medium or 3 large)
1 T. cornmeal
¾ c. sugar (or more to taste)
¼ t. salt
raisins
½ c. margarine or butter
2 eggs
½ c. milk
¼ t. nutmeg
½ t. vanilla

Cook potatoes in their skins until tender. Peel, then whip together with the remaining ingredients with mixer. Spoon into a baking dish. Bake at 350° for about 30 minutes. Yields 6 servings.

To remove the "strings" from the sweet potatoes: Before adding other ingredients, put peeled potatoes in mixing bowl. Beat; lift beaters and rinse under water. Do this about three times. A small amount of potato is lost, but not enough to matter. This method truly takes care of the strings.

Baby Baked Beans

These beans are a southern specialty, savory and delicious.

1 lb. baby lima beans
3 medium onions, cut in halves
³⁄₄ lb. dark brown sugar
1 lb. bacon

Soak beans overnight. Simmer beans with onion halves until beans are tender. Don't overcook. Drain. Layer beans, onions, brown sugar, and bacon. Bake at 325° for 3 hours. Add a little dark molasses for a little extra flavor, if desired.

Onion & Apple Casserole

Layers of apples and onions make a yummy casserole.

1½ lbs. tart apples
1 large onion
4 T. butter
2 T. brown sugar
3 T. soaked currants
³⁄₄ t. cinnamon

Peel, core, and thinly slice apples. Line bottom of a casserole dish with one-third of the apples. Coarsely chop the onion and sauté in 3 tablespoons of butter, until translucent. Turn off heat and add brown sugar, currants, and cinnamon. Put half of the mixture on top of the apples, then add one-third more apples, the rest of the onion mixture, and the remainder of apples. Dot with butter. Bake at 350° for 45 minutes. Yields 6 to 8 servings.

Green Beans with Mushroom Sauce

Top with sliced water chestnuts, peanuts, or French fried onion rings to garnish.

4 oz. mushrooms, sliced (fresh or canned)
1 small onion, diced
¼ c. butter
¼ c. flour
3 c. milk
6 oz. processed cheese, diced
⅛ t. hot pepper sauce
2 t. soy sauce
pepper to taste
1 t. seasoned salt flavor enhancer
2 pkgs. French-cut green beans, cooked

Sauté mushrooms and onion in butter for about 3 minutes. Add flour and small amount of milk, stirring so flour will not lump. Add milk, stirring as for white sauce. Add remaining ingredients except green beans. Stir sauce into green beans. Heat thoroughly.

Grandma Essie Hill's Blackberry Cobbler

This recipe dates back to 1910. It's just as tasty today as it must have been way back then!

5 c. fresh blackberries
1¼ c. plus 2 T. sugar, divided
2 c. plus 1½ T. flour, divided and sifted
½ c. plus 2 T. butter, divided
4 t. baking powder
½ t. salt
½ t. cream of tartar
½ c. milk

Toss blackberries with 1¼ cups sugar and pour them into a well-buttered 1½ quart oblong baking dish. Sprinkle with 1½ tablespoons flour and dot with 2 tablespoons of butter; set aside. Into a bowl, sift remaining flour and sugar, baking powder, salt, and cream of tartar. Cut in ½ cup butter until the mixture resembles coarse meal. With a fork, stir in milk, and form the mixture into a ball. Roll the dough out ¼-inch thick on a floured board. Cover the blackberries with the dough and trim the edges. Cut a vent in the center of the dough and sprinkle the top generously with sugar. Bake the cobbler in a 400° oven for 40 minutes or until the crust is golden. Serve warm with cream.

Scottish Shortbread

A very tender, rich cookie.

1 c. butter, softened
1 c. margarine, softened
1 c. powdered sugar
4 c. all-purpose flour
½ t. baking powder
¼ t. salt

Preheat oven to 300°. Mix butter and margarine until creamy. Gradually add the sugar. Next add the remaining dry ingredients. Turn the dough out onto counter and knead gently about 10 times. Shape into a rectangle on a large cookie sheet. Pierce at 2-inch intervals all along top of shortbread. Bake for one hour. Once properly browned, cut immediately into small rectangles. Leave in pan to cool for 10 minutes, then transfer to a wire rack to cool completely. Store in an airtight container.

At the office Christmas party, have everyone bring some canned food items so they can be donated to the food bank.

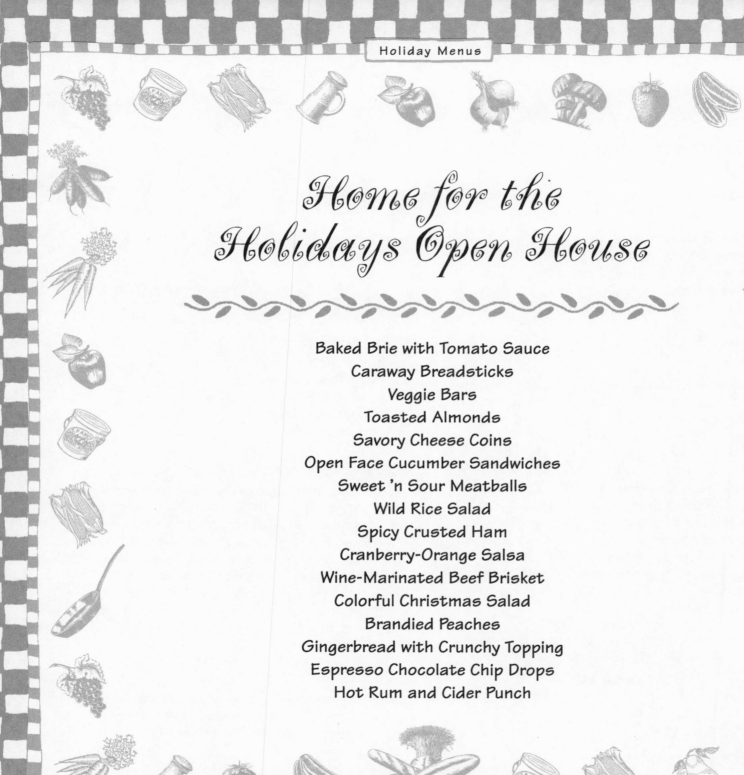

Home for the Holidays Open House

Baked Brie with Tomato Sauce
Caraway Breadsticks
Veggie Bars
Toasted Almonds
Savory Cheese Coins
Open Face Cucumber Sandwiches
Sweet 'n Sour Meatballs
Wild Rice Salad
Spicy Crusted Ham
Cranberry-Orange Salsa
Wine-Marinated Beef Brisket
Colorful Christmas Salad
Brandied Peaches
Gingerbread with Crunchy Topping
Espresso Chocolate Chip Drops
Hot Rum and Cider Punch

Baked Brie with Tomato Sauce

There's something about this Brie that brings out the fiercest of appetites!

1 frozen pastry shell, thawed
8 oz. Brie, chilled
1 T. olive oil
1 medium onion, chopped
2 garlic cloves, crushed
13-oz. can tomatoes, drained and chopped
½ T. fresh basil, chopped
1 T. fresh parsley, chopped
1 small bay leaf
salt and pepper to taste
1 T. raisins
2 T. pine nuts

With a rolling pin, flatten the pastry shell and roll out to a size that will completely cover the cheese. Wrap the cheese in the pastry, tucking the ends in snugly underneath. Make sure there are no openings in the shell. Chill the wrapped cheese for an hour. Meanwhile, heat the olive oil in a skillet and sauté the onion and garlic until tender. Stir in the remaining ingredients. Allow to simmer for 15 minutes. Place chilled cheese in a 350° oven and bake for 15 minutes, until browned. Spoon tomato sauce into a serving plate and place the cheese on top, discarding the bay leaf. Serve with crackers and caraway breadsticks.

Caraway Breadsticks

The perfect accompaniment to your baked Brie.

1 large egg, beaten
16-oz. pkg. hot roll mix
1 T. caraway seeds
1 T. coarse salt

Prepare hot roll mix, following package directions, through the kneading process. Allow dough to rest 15 minutes while you grease two cookie sheets. Divide dough into 24 pieces. On lightly floured surface, roll each piece of dough into an 8-inch-long stick and place on cookie sheet. Cover and let rise in a warm place for about 30 minutes, or until doubled in size. Heat oven as directed on hot roll mix. Brush breadsticks with beaten egg and sprinkle with caraway seeds and salt. Bake 10 to 15 minutes, or until golden. Serve warm. Yields 2 dozen.

Veggie Bars

Delicious and nutritious!

1 can crescent rolls
8 oz. cream cheese
1 c. mayonnaise
2 T. ranch dressing
6 c. raw vegetables (cauliflower, broccoli, carrots, green pepper, etc.)
Parmesan cheese

Press crescent roll dough into two 13" × 9" pans. Bake at 350° for 10 minutes. Cool crust. Mix cream cheese, mayonnaise, and ranch dressing together and place on top of crust. Chop vegetables and place on top of dressing mixture, and sprinkle with Parmesan cheese. Cut into squares.

Toasted Almonds

Spread whole almonds in a single layer in a shallow pan. Place in a cold oven; toast at 350° for 8 to 12 minutes. If you use slivered, chopped, or sliced almonds, toast only 5 to 10 minutes. Keep an eye on them, stirring occasionally until lightly toasted. Remove from pan and allow to cool. Serve as an appetizer or as a crunchy addition to salads, desserts, and main dishes. For extra flavor, add a bit of garlic salt and paprika.

Go outside, play in the snow, and come in by the fire for a cup of hot mulled cider.

Savory Cheese Coins

These make good prizes for children playing dreidel.

8 oz. sharp Cheddar cheese, shredded
½ c. butter, softened
1 c. all-purpose unbleached white flour
1 t. Worcestershire sauce
2 T. instant minced onions
pinch of cayenne pepper

Combine all ingredients in a medium bowl and mix well by hand or with a heavy-duty mixer until a dough is formed. Divide the dough in half and shape each half into a log about one inch in diameter and 12 inches long. If desired, roll in sesame seeds to coat. Wrap the logs in plastic and chill 4 hours or overnight. When logs are completely chilled, cut each log into about 48 round slices of ¼-inch thickness. Place on greased or coated baking sheets and brown in a 375° oven for 10 minutes or so. Remove coins from baking sheets to cool. Store in an airtight container. Yields 7 dozen.

Open-Face Cucumber Sandwiches

A teatime tradition from England, these cucumber sandwiches are cool and creamy.

8-oz. pkg. cream cheese
party rye bread
2 cucumbers, sliced
into thin rounds
1 pkg. dry salad
seasoning

Spread cream cheese on party rye slices and top with cucumber slices. Sprinkle with dry salad seasoning.

Sweet 'n Sour Meatballs

We just had to include this old family favorite!

1 lb. lean ground beef
1 c. soft bread crumbs
1 egg, slightly beaten
2 T. onion, minced
2 T. milk
1 clove garlic, minced
½ t. salt
⅛ t. pepper
1 T. vegetable oil
⅔ c. chili sauce
⅔ c. currant jelly
1 T. prepared mustard

Combine all ingredients except oil, chili sauce, jelly, and mustard. With wet hands, form into 40 bite-size meatballs. Brown meatballs lightly in oil. Cover and cook over low heat for 5 minutes. Drain fat. Combine chili sauce, jelly, and mustard and pour over meatballs. Heat, stirring occasionally, until jelly is melted. Simmer at least 15 minutes, until sauce has thickened, gently stirring to combine flavors. Yields 40 meatballs.

Make your favorite hot chocolate extra special. Add a scoop of vanilla ice cream. Then top with whipped cream and dust with cocoa powder. Add a cinnamon stick, and sprinkle some chocolate curls on top. Yummy!

Wild Rice Salad

A hearty, chewy, nutty side dish filled with vitamins.

2 c. wild rice, cooked
½ c. white rice, cooked
½ c. red bell pepper, diced
½ c. tomato, chopped
¼ c. green peas, cooked
¼ c. red onion, diced
¼ c. green beans, cooked and cut into pieces
4 T. frozen apple juice concentrate, thawed
2 T. red wine vinegar
2 T fresh basil, chopped
1 T. fresh parsley, chopped
1 T. fresh tarragon, chopped
1 T. fresh lime juice
salt and pepper to taste

Combine all ingredients in a large bowl, toss well, and season to taste.

Spicy Crusted Ham

The centerpiece of your holiday buffet.

5-lb. whole ham
1⅓ c. dark brown sugar, packed
¾ c. soft bread crumbs
2 t. ground mustard
½ t. ground cinnamon
½ t. black pepper, freshly ground
¼ t. ground cloves
¼ c. pineapple juice

Bake ham for one hour in a 325° oven. Remove from oven and score the top and sides. Combine sugar, bread crumbs, and spices; add juice. Mix to form a thick paste. Spread over the ham and bake another 30 minutes, or until browned. Baste with pan juices before slicing.

HOME SWEET HOME

Cranberry-Orange Salsa

A little flair from the Southwest.

2 c. dried cranberries
¾ c. fresh orange juice
1 T. orange zest, minced
⅔ c. toasted pecans
4 t. red chili powder

Purée all the ingredients in a blender or food processor. Serve with ham or turkey.

Wine-Marinated Beef Brisket

Serve with an assortment of breads and flavored mustards for sandwiches.

1 c. dry red wine
2 T. soy sauce
2 garlic cloves, minced
1 celery stalk, thinly sliced
1 small onion, grated
3 to 3½ lbs. brisket, trimmed of fat
1 medium onion, thinly sliced

Mix together the first five ingredients and put in a glass dish. Add the brisket and turn over in the marinade so it is completely coated. Cover meat and allow to marinate for a few hours in the refrigerator, turning occasionally. (If your brisket is still frozen, you can let it thaw while it sits in the marinade.) Transfer brisket to a large iron skillet and arrange the sliced onion around it. Pour half the marinade over the meat, reserving the rest. Cover the skillet with aluminum foil and roast at 325°, basting occasionally, for about 3 hours or until tender. If the meat seems to be drying out, baste with reserved marinade while it cooks. Remove from the oven and let cool a bit before you thinly slice and transfer the meat to a serving dish. Pour any pan juices over the slices. Serves about 8 as a main dish, or serve cold with sandwich buns and horseradish.

Colorful Christmas Salad

The one dish children always remember.

3-oz. pkg. lime gelatin
1 c. crushed pineapple, drained
½ c. mayonnaise
8-oz. pkg. cream cheese, softened
½ c. walnuts, chopped
3-oz. pkg. cranberry gelatin
½ c. cranberry sauce

Prepare lime gelatin as directed on package and chill until slightly thickened. Fold in pineapple. Pour into an 8-inch pan or mold and chill until firm. Combine mayonnaise and cream cheese, mixing until well blended. Add nuts and spread over molded gelatin layer. Chill until firm. Prepare cranberry gelatin and add cranberry sauce. Pour over cheese mixture and chill until firm. Remove salad by placing mold in hot water for a few minutes; then gently turn onto a serving platter.

Instead of making all your cookies from scratch, buy a mix or refrigerated dough. Assemble lots of sugars, sparkles, and colored icings and have fun!

Brandied Peaches

Also makes a special gift from your holiday kitchen.

two 29-oz. cans peach halves
1 c. sugar
½ c. peach brandy
3 drops almond extract

Drain the peaches, reserving one cup of juice. Mix the sugar with the reserved juice and boil until reduced by one-half. Cool this mixture and add the brandy and the almond extract. Pour brandy syrup over the peaches and serve, or pack peaches and brandy syrup into a sterilized one-quart glass jar and seal.

Gingerbread with Crunchy Topping

It can't be Christmas without gingerbread!

½ c. vegetable shortening
½ c. sugar
1 egg
1 c. molasses
2 ½ c. cake flour, sifted
1 ½ t. baking soda
½ t. salt
1 t. ground ginger
1 t. ground cinnamon
1 t. ground cloves
1 c. hot water

Cream shortening and sugar with an electric mixer. Add egg and beat well. Add molasses and beat well. Sift together dry ingredients. With mixer on slow speed, add dry ingredients alternately with the hot water, beating to blend. Pour batter into greased and floured 13" × 9" baking pan. Bake at 350° for 30 minutes; then sprinkle with crunchy topping. Bake 10 minutes longer, or until toothpick comes out clean. Yields 8 to 10 servings.

Crunchy Topping:
1 c. dark brown sugar, firmly packed
½ c. all-purpose flour
1 t. ground cinnamon
½ t. ground ginger
½ c. butter, cut into pieces
peel of 1 lemon, grated
1 c. pecans or walnuts, chopped

Combine sugar, flour, cinnamon, and ginger in a bowl. With pastry blender or two knives, cut butter into mixture until it resembles coarse meal. Mix in lemon peel and nuts. Sprinkle mixture over gingerbread 10 minutes before the end of baking time.

Espresso Chocolate Chip Drops

The perfect after-dinner treat!

32 milk chocolate drops
2/3 c. butter-flavored shortening
1/2 c. granulated sugar
1/2 c. light brown sugar, firmly packed
1 egg
1 T. milk
1 t. pure vanilla extract
1/2 t. brandy extract
1 1/2 c. all-purpose flour
1 t. ground French-roast espresso coffee
1/2 t. baking soda
1/4 t. salt
1/2 c. chopped walnuts (optional)
1/3 c. semisweet chocolate chips
1/3 c. milk chocolate chips

Preheat oven to 375°. Remove foil wrappers from candies. Combine shortening, sugars, egg, milk, vanilla, and brandy extract in a large bowl. Beat at medium speed with electric mixer until well blended. Combine flour, ground coffee, soda, and salt. Gradually add to creamed mixture at low speed, beating until blended well. Stir in nuts, semisweet, and milk chocolate chips with spoon. Drop batter by slightly rounded teaspoonfuls 2 inches apart onto ungreased cookie sheet. Bake for 8 to 10 minutes or until light brown and just set. Do not overbake. Place one chocolate candy in center of each cookie. Cool one to 2 minutes on baking sheet before removing cookies. Yields 32 cookies.

Hot Rum & Cider Punch

Goes well with gingerbread or pumpkin pie!

1 qt. apple cider
2 T. maple syrup
2 T. sugar
4 oz. fresh lemon juice
1 qt. light rum
1 lemon, sliced into
    12 pieces
12 whole cloves
12 cinnamon sticks

Heat the cider and stir in syrup and sugar. Add lemon juice and rum; garnish with lemon slices stuck with cloves. Place a cinnamon stick in each cup. Yields 12 servings.

Index

A

APPETIZERS

Toasted Almonds, 136
Baked Brie with Tomato
   Sauce, 135
Bean Dip, 72
Caraway Breadsticks, 135
Cheese Sausage Squares, 72
Country Cheese & Cider
   Spread, 71
Crab Puffs, 74
Crab Quiche, 128
Ham & Swiss Rolls, 73
Hot Pecan Dip, 72
Mushroom Logs, 129
Mushrooms Florentine, 74
Open-Face Cucumber
   Sandwiches, 137
Rudolph's Nose Herbal Chili
   Ball, 73
Stromboli, 80
Sweet 'n Sour Meatballs, 137
Veggie Bars, 136
Yuletide Crab Puffs, 74

B

BAR COOKIES

Chocolate Chip Cream
   Cheese Bars, 101
Holiday Chocolate Bars, 38
Lemon Chess, 100
Patrick's Chocolate Brownies,
   102
Seven-Layer Bars, 101

BEEF

Busy Day Casserole, 77
Christmas Meatloaf, 79
Corned Beef & Cabbage, 86
Hash, 85
Prime Rib Roast, 114
Roast in Sherry, 86
Sweet 'n Sour Meatballs, 137
Wine-Marinated Brisket, 139

BEVERAGES

Christmas Wassail, 121
Holiday Cocoa, 40
Hot Rum & Cider Punch, 141
Mulled Cranberry Cider, 128
Mulling Spice Bags, 43
Smiling Bishops, 121
Sunrise Punch, 123
Vanilla Coffee, 123

BREADS AND MUFFINS

Applesauce Muffins, 123
Apricot Nut Bread, 36
Caraway Breadsticks, 135
Christmas Morning Sticky
   Buns, 126
Date & Pumpkin Loaves, 41
Eggnog Cherry Muffins, 75
Jalapeño Cornbread, 75
Pumpkin Nut Bread, 126
Stromboli, 80

BREAKFAST

Casseroles, 79, 87, 124
Christmas Breakfast Strata,
   87
Honey Spiced Ham, 125
Mel's Christmas Morning
   Casserole, 87
Overnight Egg Omelet, 88
Skiers' French Toast, 124
Warm Country Gingerbread
   Waffles, 88

C

CAKES

Chocolate Torte, 100
Christmas Cheesecake, 106
Heavenly Black Forest, 108
Gingerbread with Crunchy
   Topping, 140
Holiday Gift, 37
Merry Berry Almond Glazed
   Sour Cream, 109
Mom's Carrot, 108
Old-Fashioned Fruitcake, 104
Walnut Torte, 120

CANDIES AND CONFECTIONS

Candied Oranges, 118
Christmas Truffles, 43
Homemade Caramels, 39
Peanut Brittle, 38
Spiced Pecans, 41

CASSEROLES

Breakfast, 79, 87, 124
Broccoli, 117
Busy Day, 77
Chicken Divine, 82
Enid's Spinach-Cheese, 78
Ham 'n Turkey, 78
Onion & Apple, 132
Mel's Christmas Morning, 87
Sweet Potato, 131
Yankee Pleaser, 79

CHEESE

Baked Brie with Tomato
   Sauce, 135
Broccoli Casserole, 117
Busy Day Casserole, 77
Cheese Sausage Squares, 72
Chocolate Chip Cream
   Cheese Bars, 101
Christmas Cheesecake, 106

CHEESE (*continued*)
Country Cheese & Cider Spread, 71
Crab Quiche Appetizers, 128
Enid's Spinach-Cheese Casserole, 78
Ham & Swiss Rolls, 73
Jalapeño Cornbread, 75
Overnight Egg Omelet, 88
Rudolph's Nose Herbal Chili Ball, 73
Savory Cheese Coins, 136
Stromboli, 80

CHICKEN
Breasts Chablis, 82
Breasts with Champagne Sauce, 80
Divine, 82
Orange, 81

COOKIES
Banny's Southern Cream, 94
Better-than-Tollhouse Chocolate Chip Hearts, 103
Carrot Chip, 42
Christmas Cranberry Roll-Up, 89
Coconut Meringue, 93
Crispy Oatmeal, 92
Elves' Belly Buttons, 98
Espresso Chocolate Chip Drops, 141
Farmhouse Chocolate Mint, 95
Frosted Party, 96
Gingerbread, 95
Gingerbread Babies, 36
I Love Shortbread, 93
Lace Roll-Ups, 99
Lemon Snowdrops, 90
Maple Nut, 94

COOKIES (*continued*)
Night Before Christmas Mice, 98
Orange Iced Cranberry, 97
Peanut Butter, with Icing, 91
Rudolph, 92
Rum Balls, 98
Scottish Shortbread, 133
Snickerdoodles, 97
Stained-Glass, 92
See also Bars

CORNISH HENS
Cranberry-Orange Glazed, 81

CRAFTS, 24-35
Advent Chain, 34
Bird Food, 25
Candy Cane Door Prizes, 31
Casserole Cozies, 34
Christmas Cards, 24, 28
Christmas Wrap, 31, 33
Dried Cranberry Heart, 26
Easy Christmas Tree Lapel Pin, 35
Fabric Gift Bags, 27
Family Fun Surprise Jar, 28
Family Treasures, 26
Framed Picture Ornaments, 27
Gift Baskets, 30, 33
Gift Box Advent Calendar, 32
Gift Tags, 29
Grandparents' Gift, 28
Photo Wrap, 31
Potpourri
Ornaments, 35
Sachet, 34
Yuletide, 25
Recipe Box, 30
Scented Bath Salts, 29
Scented Pinecone Baskets, 30

CRAFTS (*continued*)
Soap Stars, 25
Tree Ornaments, 12-15, 35
Tree Skirt, 15
Tweet Hearts, 25
Twinkling Grapevine Spheres, 31

DECORATIONS, 16-21, 59

DESSERTS
Apple Grunt, 99
Brandied Peaches, 140
Brownie Trifle, 103
Grandma Essie Hill's Blackberry Cobbler, 133
Grandma's Apple Crisp, 90
Mint-Filled Chocolate Cups, 119
Out-of-this-World Fudge Topping, 106
See also Bars; Cakes; Cookies; Pies

DRESSING
Mother's Celery Cornbread, 131

HAM
Baked with Cherry Glaze, 129
Ham & Swiss Rolls, 73
Ham 'n Turkey Casserole, 78
Honey Spiced, 125
Spicy Crusted, 138

JAMS & JELLIES
Hot Pepper Jelly, 40
Orange-Cranberry Marmalade, 39

NUTS
Creamed Onions with Peanuts, 114
Spiced Pecans, 41
Toasted Almonds, 136

PIES
The Best Apple Walnut Raisin, 105
Get Your Moose Chocolate Style, 107
Grandma Liz's Pumpkin, 104
Not-So-Sweet Pecan, 105
PUDDING, Yorkshire, 114

RELISHES
Cranberry-Orange Chutney, 125
Cranberry-Orange Salsa, 138
Pears with Cranberry Relish, 117

SALADS
Christmas Crunch, 76
Colorful Christmas, 139
Easy Artichoke Rice, 76
Frozen Christmas, 118
Wild Rice, 138

SAUSAGE
Breakfast Casseroles, 79, 87, 124
Cheese Squares, 72
Christmas Breakfast Strata, 87
Zucchini Soup, 71
SHELLFISH
Christmas Luncheon Crabmeat Bisque, 84
Clam Chowder, 70
Crab Puffs, 74
Crab Quiche Appetizers, 128
Shrimp Scampi, 84
SOUPS, CHOWDERS & BISQUES
Christmas Luncheon Crabmeat Bisque, 84
Clam Chowder, 70
Corn Chowder, 70
Easy Velvet Broccoli Soup, 71
Zucchini Sausage, 71
SPICES
Mulling Spice Bags, 43

TRADITIONS, 44-67
TREE ORNAMENTS, 12-15, 35
TURKEY
Ham 'n Turkey Casserole, 78
Juciest-Ever Roast, 130

VEGETABLES
Baked Artichokes with Mustard Butter Sauce, 113
Baby Baked Beans, 132
Broccoli Casserole, 117
Corn Chowder, 70

Corned Beef & Cabbage, 86
Creamed Onions with Peanuts, 114
Easy Cheese-Scalloped Potatoes, 85
Easy Velvet Broccoli Soup, 71
Glazed Carrots, 115
Green Beans with Mushroom Sauce, 132
Lentil and Mushroom Loaf with Savory Potato Filling, 116
Mother's Celery Cornbread Dressing, 131
Mushroom Logs, 129
Mushrooms Florentine, 74
Onion & Apple Casserole, 132
Open-Face Cucumber Sandwiches, 137
Sour Cream Mashed Potatoes, 115
Spinach-Cheese Casserole, 78
Sweet Potato Casserole, 131
Vegetable Chili, 83
Veggie Bars, 136
Zucchini Sausage Soup, 71
VINEGARS
Thyme, Lemon Peel, & Black Pepper, 42